PRESTON SCOTT COHEN
TAIYUAM MUSEUM OF ART

PRESTON SCOTT COHEN
TAIYUAN MUSEUM OF ART

SOURCE BOOKS IN ARCHITECTURE

KNOWLTON SCHOOL OF ARCHITECTURE
THE OHIO STATE UNIVERSITY
BENJAMIN WILKE, SERIES EDITOR

11

a r + d
APPLIED
RESEARCH
+DESIGN
PUBLISHING

Preston Scott Cohen: Taiyuan Museum of Art
Source Books in Architecture 11
Benjamin Wilke, Series Editor

Knowlton School of Architecture
The Ohio State University
Applied Research+Design Publishing, San Francisco

Published by Applied Research and Design Publishing.
Gordon Goff: Publisher

www.appliedresearchanddesign.com
info@appliedresearchanddesign.com

Book Design: Pablo Mandel / CircularStudio.com
Typeset in Akzidenz-Grotesk Pro

10 9 8 7 6 5 4 3 2 1 First Edition

ISBN: 978-1-939621-58-0

Project Manager: Jake Anderson
Color Separations and Printing: AR+D Publishing.
Printed in China.

AR+D Publishing makes a continuous effort to minimize the overall carbon
footprint of its publications. As part of this goal, AR+D Publishing, in
association with Global ReLeaf, arranges to plant trees to replace those used
in the manufacturing of the paper produced for its books. Global ReLeaf is
an international campaign run by American Forests, one of the world's oldest
nonprofit conservation organizations. Global ReLeaf is American Forests'
education and action program that helps individuals, organizations, agencies,
and corporations improve the local and global environment by planting and
caring for trees.

Contents

Source Books in Architecture

Following the example of music publication, Source Books in Architecture offers an alternative to the traditional architectural monograph. If one is interested in hearing music, he or she simply buys the desired recording. If, however, one wishes to study a particular piece in greater depth, it is possible to purchase the score—the written code that more clearly elucidates the structure, organization, and creative process that brings the work into being. This series is offered in the same spirit. Each Source Book focuses on the work of a particular architect or on a special topic in contemporary architecture and is meant to expose the foundations and details of the work in question. The work is documented through sketches, models, renderings, working drawings, writings, and photographs at a level of detail that allows complete and careful study of a project from conception to completion. The graphic component is accompanied by commentary from the architect and critics that further explore the technical and cultural content of the work.

Source Books in Architecture was conceived by Jeffrey Kipnis and Robert Livesey and is the product of the Herbert Baumer seminars, a series of interactions between students and seminal practitioners at the Knowlton School of Architecture at the Ohio State University. After a significant amount of research on the Herbert Baumer Distinguished Visiting Professor, students lead a discussion that encourages those architects to reveal their motives and techniques. The meetings are recorded and transcribed and become the basis for these Source Books.

The seminars are made possible by a generous bequest from Herbert Herndon Baumer. Educated at the École des Beaux-Arts, Baumer was a professor in the Department of Architecture at the Ohio State University from 1922 to 1956. He had a dual career as a distinguished design professor who inspired many students and as a noted architect who designed several buildings at the Ohio State University and other Ohio colleges.

Acknowledgments

Preston Scott Cohen's *Contested Symmetries* was the first publication that I bought as a graduate student. I remember still how alien and precise the work seemed to me at the time and the degree to which it expanded my understanding of the breadth of architectural inquiry and production. Thank you to Preston Scott Cohen for allowing me an inside look at his processes and ideas. It has been a pleasure to work with someone whose energy and acuity carry such dedication and depth.

Thank you to the friends and colleagues who contributed to the content of this book: Stan Allen, Kristy Balliet, Doug Graf, Jeff Kipnis, and Rob Livesey. I am truly thankful for the efforts that everyone put forth in the midst of busy schedules.

At the Knowlton School of Architecture, Rob Livesey and Mike Cadwell have and continue to be tremendously supportive of the Source Books in Architecture series and provide constant advice and enthusiasm. Thanks to Lisa Wareham and Carla Sharon (and the whole of the Knowlton administrative team) for their energy and help whenever needed. Special thanks to Aaron Powers for his initial transcription of Preston Scott Cohen's Baumer Sessions text.

Thank you to Gordon Goff and Jake Anderson at ORO Editions for their assistance and expertise, and to Pablo Mandel of Circular Studio for his design efforts and patience.

INTRODUCTION

Stan Allen

Preston Scott Cohen and I belong to a generation schooled in the idea of drawing as the "perfect" act of architecture. In my case, as a student at the Cooper Union in the early 1980s, I was confronted with the figure of John Hejduk, for whom fully realized architectural ideas could be described by drawings alone. But while Hejduk built very little, the act of building remained at the center of his practice. His projects were drawn with an attention to detail and a tectonic precision that allowed them to be faithfully executed by others. Not so with Hejduk's most prominent student, Daniel Libeskind, who had studied at Cooper Union a decade earlier. In the early stages of his career, Libeskind pursued the idea of an architecture that could begin and end in drawing, free of all constraint. Ironically, it was Libeskind's contemporary, Leon Krier, in the late 1970s, who articulated the most extreme version of this position: "I don't build because I am an architect. I can make true architecture because I do not build." Krier and Libeskind had little else in common, but they were unified in their distrust of the compromise and commercialism that building practice implied. For these architects (as with Hejduk, Peter Eisenman, and Raimund Abraham, among others) a "true architecture" was only possible in the idealized realm of representation.[1]

The most forceful counter-argument is found in the writings of Rafael Moneo. In his essay "The Solitude of Buildings" (1985), Moneo insists that ideas about architecture cannot be divorced from their material realization. "Architecture," he writes, "needs the support of matter." He contrasts the "tyranny of drawings" with the "crude reality of built works," preferring the hard discipline of the latter. For Moneo, a finished building is a silent thing in the world, independent of its author, having left behind the contingencies of its design and construction. "I do not believe that architecture is just the superstructure that we introduce when we talk about buildings. I prefer to think that architecture is the air we breathe when buildings have arrived at their radical solitude." Buildings, in this account, take on a life of their own and do not belong exclusively to the architect. Underlying this debate is the distinction articulated by Kenneth Frampton between the representational and the tectonic (or the "scenographic" and the "ontological"). For Frampton, as for Moneo, architecture's capacity to communicate—to operate within a cultural sphere of reference—is less significant than its existential condition as a thing among things in the world: a grounded ontology of place, tectonics, materiality, and lived experience.

These polemics, which shaded the atmosphere of our education, can seem distant today. Eisenman has consistently realized large-scale works and Libeskind maintains an active building practice. But their buildings often appear as direct transcriptions of drawn experiments; even as built works they remain in the realm of representation. (Famously, in the case of Eisenman's House 2, the architect was quite happy that photographs of the built work were mistaken for photographs of a model). The material realization has changed but the gap between representation and construction remains.

Preston Scott Cohen studied at RISD with Judy Wolin and Rodolfo Machado, and at Harvard with Peter Eisenman. Scott Cohen's earliest published works were a series of houses that managed the difficult trick of reconciling seemingly incompatible source material: domestic iconicity inspired by Venturi, perhaps by way of his years at RISD, overlaid with process-based formal deformations and displacements, which recalled Rowe and Eisenman. Drawn by hand in limpid perspectives, the effect of these uncanny hybrids was both strange and original. They anticipated their own realization as built works (which unfortunately did not happen), as much as they foreshadowed Scott Cohen's future design preoccupations and built works.

I think it's fair to say that for Scott Cohen and myself, these debates of an older generation could only lead to a dead end. Attracted as much by the intricacies of design process as by the self-evident presence of construction, to choose between building and drawing seemed a false dilemma. In different ways, and shaped by different experiences, we were both looking for a conceptual and practice model that might bridge that gap in a productive way.

This background—and the intellectual impasse it threatened—helps explain a shared fascination with the writings of Robin Evans, which have served several generations of architects as a template to rethink drawing practice. For Evans, the identifying characteristic of architectural drawing is precisely its capacity to translate between drawing and building. Architecture's long history of representation is marked by the shuttling back and forth between the abstract two-dimensional condition of drawing and the concrete three-dimensional reality of the building. For Evans, drawing is fundamental to architecture, but his understanding of drawing is not based on linguistic theories of representation. It is instead operative and instrumental. In the final chapter of *The Projective Cast* he clearly states his skepticism of the linguistic model: "Architecture, which remodels nature on the pattern of geometry's fabricated truths, is just one step outside the circle of signs. If we insist that architecture is a code, divesting it of all its obdurate, thinglike qualities at a stroke, it is easily drawn back into that circle and we are alleviated of further responsibility to explain its relation to other events that do not show up so well in the endless chains of representation" (Evans 355). For Evans, who once wrote that "Projection could be considered the universal ether of constructability" (357), representation is not something added onto building, but that which makes architecture possible in the first place. The "projective cast" is the ephemeral shadow of geometry cast on the obstinate ground of reality. His emphasis on the long, difficult, and conservative labor of translation differentiates him from those who (like Eisenman or Libeskind) would see building as the direct registration of geometric complexity. But by emphasizing the fluidity and instability of architecture's graphic instruments, Evans also distances his arguments from those (like Frampton) who advocate a return to the ontology of construction. For Evans, the tectonic and the graphic are not necessarily opposed, and Scott Cohen has taken this insight to heart. He has elaborated on Evans's close attention to the transmissive properties of projection, and in particular the use of the ruled surface and stereotomy. These are key moments when tectonic and graphic coincide: crude matter follows the dictates of geometry. Scott Cohen has built a distinctive design language on the convergence of geometry and construction. His work reminds us that architecture is a complex intellectual labor, carried out with highly specific tools, and at the same time, it is never reducible to the catalogue of those tools or techniques.

As the work assembled here demonstrates, Scott Cohen takes equal pleasure in design process— drawings, computer modeling, and the play of projective geometries—as he does in all of those effects that are only possible in a realized building: light and shadow; the changing parallax of a spectator moving through actual space; materials and details. He understands the exquisite satisfaction (that belongs only to architecture) of making a place that takes on a life of its own and becomes part of the life of the city and its citizens. His practice has been transformed from those early days by the use of contemporary digital tools and larger-scale commissions, but something of these essential enabling insights remain as he continues to work seamlessly between the fluidity of geometry and the stubborn reality of building.

Notes

1. Kipnis – Perfect Acts – by 2001 already a historical phenomenon…

BAUMER SESSIONS

The following text was extracted from a series of conversations between Preston Scott Cohen, Kristy Balliet, and the students of the Knowlton School of Architecture during the 2014-2015 school year.

A NARROW ESCAPE

PRESTON SCOTT COHEN: My first teaching job was here at Ohio State, a very particular place in my history and a good starting point from which to explain how some of the ideas came to be. I was twenty-seven when I began teaching here. I didn't have much credibility. I had been out of school (RISD followed by the GSD) for just three years during which I had been working for firms in New York and moonlighting much more enthusiastically on the early series of unbuilt houses. Jeff Kipnis invited me to teach and while here I became very close to Doug Graf. Their work was important to me. Rob Livesey, the dean, and the faculty were excellent. The school was a remarkable place to be and I wanted to continue teaching here.

Jeff and Rob seemed at once intent on intimidating me and on keeping me here. At the end of two terms of teaching, I was going for a long-term position. I was a finalist, up for an interview, and Jeff Kipnis kept saying, "You better be ready, we're going to have tough questions." I set incredibly high standards for myself. My reaction to all of this was to freeze. By the weekend before the interview, I had reached a state of absolute paralysis, unable to prepare a presentation.

The interview was scheduled for a Monday morning. Just thirty minutes before, the phone rang and I found myself listening intently to the almost undecipherable accent of Rafael Moneo saying, "I want to bring you to Harvard. Don't let Jeff be angry with me but this is what has to happen." I was living near campus in a delightfully dumpy apartment on Chittenden Avenue. I ran as quickly as I could from there to Rob's office, arriving just minutes before the interview was supposed to start only to tell him that I wasn't going to proceed with it after all. The narrow escape from this dreaded interrogation was one of the happiest moments of my life. I'll never know what they would have asked me or done

with me. I'm turning white just thinking about it! So why do I bring up Ohio State?

KRISTY BALLIET: Where it all began …

WHAT ARCHITECTURE IS

COHEN: When I was teaching at Ohio State, I became preoccupied with a little quirk I had noticed, which was that many good architects had decided to state what architecture *is*. Peter Eisenman claimed that architecture is *the sign signifying another thing demarcating the sign*. I don't remember, exactly. Venturi wrote that architecture is a struggle between the inside and the outside. For Le Corbusier, architecture is *the masterly, correct, and magnificent play of masses brought together in light*. Kahn thought that architecture is what the brick wants to be. With his *less is more*, Mies considered architectural quality quantitatively. For Sullivan, it was *form follows function*. Years later, I found out that Philip Johnson thought that architecture is *the art of wasting space*. It didn't follow function but rather exceeded it. By then, I had grown to feel very sympathetic to Sullivan's definition. Now, I would say that Johnson's and Venturi's are the truest and most endemic to architecture.

One of my own definitions, "architecture is a betrayal of geometry," doesn't include enough of the things that matter most to me, but nonetheless captures another idea that I regard to be significant. The idea of distortion, which is of enormous importance and about which I will speak later, plays a significant role in this. Architecture distorts geometry and, in turn, geometry distorts architecture.

As opposed to geometry, Le Corbusier thought the plan was the generator of architecture. This is such a brilliant idea. He thought that a new architecture would come from rethinking and reinventing the plan and that we would regenerate everything by drawing the plan first. What he was criticizing implicitly is the idea that the form of buildings preexisted the plan. When you think of a classical temple, you know the plan. You basically know the temple as a type and the plan is given. There's nothing to invent. It's not generated by the plan. Instead, an idea, a principal, a paradigm, and a mental construct were the generators. The classical canon. It's already given to you and you don't need to generate it. The idea that you generate anything is profoundly radical.

I think we've passed the phase in which we understood the plan to be a generator. We have actually returned to the earlier tradition: the plan as given. The form is what we model and the form gives us the plan. It used to be that the model preexisted us because it came from the temple or from some other type—a panopticon, for example. No, now we've made up the form so you can say the model is the generator. We'll call it *modeling as the generator of architecture*. And only after the fact do we have the plan. We are back to the plan as being after the fact, just as it was before Le Corbusier.

In the medieval period the plan *did* generate architecture. The building originated from a plan drawn on the ground. No one had a complete preconception of what would rise from the plan.

The other definition that I propose, "architecture is the distortion of buildings," suggests that buildings are the medium of architecture. Buildings are to architecture what paint is to painting. Le Corbusier's idea that architecture exists when the window or the door is too large or too small—i.e., when it's not normal—is obviously closely related to this idea. He's referring to the element that is familiar and to the size that we know it to properly be. To have architecture, you must have the norm and you must have the exception to the norm.

Peter Eisenman brought this idea of Le Corbusier's to my attention. Peter always liked the idea of architecture turning into a language; he liked the idea of a window operating as a signifier. It wasn't so much that it was about a norm and an exception as much as it was the idea that everything could be turned into a word referring to another word.

And yet, I was actually more interested in Venturi's preoccupation with vernacular architecture, a language of peculiar anomalies. There are occasions when it becomes architecture in Venturi's mind because it is breaking from the norm. I have to give him credit for that idea, even though he doesn't use those exact words. For him, the signals that things are sending—compositionally—are complicated. Venturi doesn't think architecture should be reduced to a modern functional ideology where everything is rationalized and given a certain kind of clarity that would absolve architecture of making a mess. He liked the messiness of reality. He was trying to return architecture to the common world by allowing all of the mess to be a part of it. Venturi is really important because he's looking at modernity and he's dealing with its production and materials. He's dealing with the thinness of architecture and he's not trying to make a classical building. He's like Eisenman. He wants to make architecture some kind of signifier.

But what did this leave me with? Making windows that are too big or too small? Making gables that were too steep or shallow? Making hip roofs that were a little bit peculiar? Just making abstract ambiguous shapes? The latter was a version of impressionism that didn't interest me because it wasn't part of the discourse about normativity and distortion. It wasn't any kind of discourse at all. It was just form.

I told Greg Lynn last week in a conference to please admit that architecture is over for him. It's not of interest to him. Le Corbusier wrote that architecture is a machine for living in, a grounded ocean liner adrift in the landscape. Architecture manifests itself in decidedly discreet entities. Indeed, his Marseille block appears as one, a ship with the chimneys, etcetera (1). Instead of taking the ship out of the water and making architecture out of it, Greg is putting architecture in the water. Why should a building act like it's moving in water? This is a case of desiring to make a building act like it's confronting forces that it doesn't confront. I talked about necessity earlier. In lieu of lawfulness, I need geometry and function to lend architecture authority and Greg needs water. He needs the forces that act on boats because he can't do anything purposefully without them. It just isn't interesting enough, otherwise. I should grant him the fact that he is expanding the repertoire by playing with these forces. The problem is that he claims that architecture should literally be derived from them.

Diller + Scofidio's folded shirts—a piece called "Bad Press"—is architectural (2), moreso than Greg

Lynn's yacht (3). The shirts are, in my opinion, their best work. They basically used an iron to distort rather than to rectify a shirt. The iron is a projective instrument that flattens and creases. They associated it with a wider culture of the hygienic, sterilized, mass-produced dress shirt that is, of course, the male subjects' primary formal attire. The female subjects' role in the maintenance of it in that form is also related to a codified, subversive system that exists in prisons. Supplementary creases can be added as markings to signal alliances among prisoners and to plan escapes. The creases were secret codes. The communicative creases were purposeful. What do their own uselessly exceptional creases mean?

For me, architecture is constituted by buildings that contain institutional programs. This is a precondition that distinguishes architecture. Today, in many schools, several people take the poetic stance that architecture is not just buildings: it's writing, it's theorization, it's anthropology. It's everything. There seems to be an expanding repertoire of what constitutes architecture. Why am I interested in the incorrectly ironed shirt and in ideas that come from various films? Because I am interested in argumentation. Like Warhol's film *Sleep*, *Bad Press* is revelatory for architecture, but it's not architecture. This is a very important distinction. We couldn't have architecture without writing. You can't have an idea about architecture without other mediums to describe it. So I think it's dependent on the other mediums, but it is not the same thing as *being* them.

ARCHITECTURAL ANAMORPHOSIS

How does anamorphosis manifest itself in architecture? A few years prior to the work on projective geometry, during the summer after I taught at OSU, I went to Italy and tracked down Villa Tauro (4). I had discovered Tauro in the library here, in a survey of mostly anonymous buildings in the Veneto. I had been attracted to certain kinds of deviations from symmetry in fenestration patterns ever since having found one villa, in particular, outside of Assisi back in 1981. What I loved about Tauro was the central area of the facade that was obviously disturbed.

I discovered the cause for Tauro's distortion, which is precisely what makes it so interesting. There were three equal rooms in plan. Between two, a stair had been inserted (5). The way stairs were usually inserted

into this type of villa at the time—perpendicular to the main axis—would, to varying degrees, leave the overall symmetry of the plan undisturbed. Palladio thought staircases should disappear. Otherwise, they were disruptive elements. The only stair you could ever exhibit would be the grand ceremonial entry—or the stair *up* in the base of the villa as if it were a temple—but never the internal communicative stairs from level to level. The formal spaces of Palladio's buildings were all on one level. There was absolutely no vertical succession (or stacking of spaces). His architecture was only successive horizontally from room to room. You'd move laterally and any stair was suppressed by being buried in the poche, whether it be a stair to the cellar, a stair to the attic, or a stair to the servant's quarters.

The stair at Villa Tauro is inserted in such a way that it forces the middle room to be compressed and attenuated. The effort to conceal this anomaly strains the building's facade and landscape. It is as if the villa is aiming to restore itself to symmetry despite the stair that messes up the facade. In my analysis at the time, I realized something that is so much more compelling than the projective drawings: this villa's facade was analogous to anamorphosis. When you're looking at an instance of anamorphosis, such as Holbein's *The Ambassadors* (6), you see a very distorted figure overlaid on a normal pictorial space. You see an unrecognizably distorted figure floating over the image. It turns out that if you look at this figure from the far left edge of the painting, it's a perfectly projected image of a skull. This distortion hides a message, which is that the king is mortal. This was an important example for me because I wanted architecture to possess meaningful distortion. I wanted an architecture that was both normal and distorted.

Anyway, here comes Villa Tauro and its symmetry is disturbed for a very different reason than the distortion that occurs in *the Ambassadors*: the Palladian imperative to repress the internal stair. While writing *Contested Symmetries*, I grew to love the fact that the stair was a functional and necessary organ of the building. I loved that the cause of the disruption of symmetry was not voluntary. It was not distortion for distortion's sake. In this case, the distortion was brought about by the necessity to include and deny the presence of the stairway. It looks like the architect had to do it, if only to remain true to the tripartite principle of the plan. In fact, there could have

1

4

2

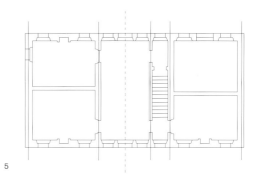

5

3

6

been a deep plan like those of other villas, wherein the stair would have been off to the side in one of the two side bays, a type of plan that enabled the middle bay to be free and clear and with all three bays of the same width (7). This type of tripartite plan, with the switch back stair in a side bay, is consistent with the Venetian palazzo type where only the side elevation would exhibit the odd condition of fenestration on the half level produced by the stair landing (8). Tauro's architect decided to make the building only one room deep, so narrow that there was no other solution than to make the stair a single run placed perpendicularly to the main facade. On the facade, the stair is deftly camouflaged by an additional narrow bay inserted between two of the main three. Given that this villa is so small, there's only one stair and natural selection would tell us that it's going to be on one side or the other of the central bay. It happens to be on the right.

What is strange is that the architect was determined to have a stair within a plan that was too tight to accept it and so constrained and basic as to be reducible to three equal parts. He made it impossible to put a stair in without messing it up and then proceeded to mess it up and to mend it. This is a very strange and productively distortive way to do things that remains important to me to this day.

That stair is the equivalent of Holbein's skull; its meaning is hidden. What the architect does so brilliantly is to squeeze the middle part of the plan and to introduce a new bay of windows that is so complicatedly associated with the other windows as to appear not to be there, depending on how you look at the overall facade. If you pay attention to only the center of the villa, the added bay seems to be part of the side bay. If you look at the two side bays, it seems to be a part of the center. Whichever way you look at the building—depending on how you think about it and how you focus your attention on the fenestration—that stair is generating a rupture in the symmetry in one of several different ways.

But this example is *not* like the anamorphism of painting in another important way. Painting assumes a fixed point of view, meaning that when you are looking at it frontally, your position in space is presumably fixed. Unlike architecture, except with wall murals, you do not view painting in a state of distraction or in a state of constant movement. The beauty of anamorphic projection is that when you move, what looks attenuated or foreshortened appears to change. In the case of Villa Tauro, the perception of its symmetry depends on how you approach the facade from the landscape.

Ultimately, Tauro's distortion of symmetry is caused by the stairs … a function that disturbed the villa's spatial equilibrium. Function is the essence of this distortion, not vision and—in my mind—this is what makes the example of Villa Tauro, as opposed to the projective drawings, a superior way to think about distortion in architecture. The flat fish (9) exemplifies a distortion that is caused by its habitat: the shallow waters in which it must swim. The fish changes between the days of its youth and maturity. Buildings also change with time. The flat fish is still a perfect allegory of our projects. It's projected. It's disfigured by necessity. We identify with this fish. We know that it should be symmetrical, but isn't.

BALLIET: The text that we looked at where we really dove into those issues was *Regular Anomalies*. We ended up talking a bit more about San Carlo ai Catinari (10) than we did some of the palazzos, but I think it's a similar condition. It's about resolving the anomaly within the poche as opposed to on the interior or the exterior.

COHEN: Yes, exactly. But that building also has a facade of unstable patterns of fenestration. I was drawn to San Carlo when I was in Rome in the late '90s. I thought that the symmetry was only disturbed in the facade. Then I realized that the corner of the building is pierced by an elliptical cylinder. This turned out to mean that projection could solve a problem: the need to maintain symmetry while bringing light into the building in a stealthy, mystical manner. Again, concealment was of the essence. Hence, the first project that I gave to the students at the GSD called "The Hidden Room" taught concealment to be among the salient motivations for architecture.

The pierced corner allowed for the transmission of light from sources that were not made clear from the interior. It allowed for dealing with the fact that the source of light was on a corner and that the fenestration limited the possibilities for where the openings through the corner could be. What I love is that projection solves the problem and distorts the building by doing so. Before this realization, my interest in projection was mainly about the appearance of distortion and the expansion of the vocabulary of architecture. With San

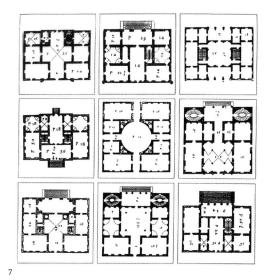

7

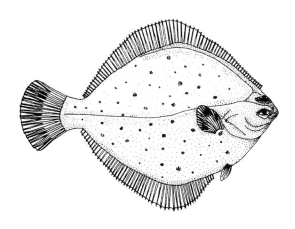

9

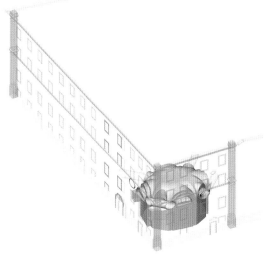

10 The Tubular Embrasure of San Carlo ai Catinari, Preston Scott Cohen, 2000

8

Carlo, projection became the dialectic of function and form that matters most.

EARLY PROJECTS

The situation in architecture today is considerably different than it was twenty-five years ago. At the time, the repertoire of forms and the language of architecture seemed to be limited by the historicism of post-modernism and the fragmentation of deconstruction. I was always interested in something that seemed more involuntary.

My teaching at OSU was very much related to the early houses. The Longboat Key House (11) was Venturi plus Eisenman plus Le Corbusier. You know how Venturi has gables that are strangely distorted? What I did was to combine distortion and abstraction. I doubled the gable and thus was dealing with problematic syntax questions like the ones that Eisenman was interested in. So there were two grids that were 90 degrees to one another. One gable was on the front of the house and the other was turned 90 degrees on the inside. I superimposed the two of them, fused them, and distorted them. Venturi would never compositionally superimpose forms or grids, or fuse or transform.

The Siesta Key House (12) led me to the search for the villas in the Veneto. Its facade was dualistic or tri-partite depending on how you looked at it. Frontally, the surface appears to be dominated by two large windows. From the far right side, you can see a third equally-distanced, hidden in a reveal the width of a staircase.

The breakthrough project was the Cornered House (13). Cornered House is trying to reinvent the American suburban domestic vernacular through projective geometry. It expands the language of normativity by distorting it beyond anything you've ever seen while retaining enough of the common traits so as to be still oddly familiar. It's still a gable and it's still a hip roof, but it's been sheared, folded, and tilted. It's like a still life of vernacular architecture in a cubistic, yet three-dimensional rendition. It is a premonition of the Tel Aviv Museum (14). The Fahmy House in Los Gatos is the topographically-necessitated version of the tilt (15).

BALLIET: In terms of successive architecture, when we looked at the Cornered House there's the idea of it connecting to the adjacent suburban houses. We now talk about how the individual buildings of urban successive architecture do not necessarily have a connection to what is around them. Yet, clearly, this is an attempt to have a building connect to its adjacent conditions.

COHEN: Of course, though the site is fictional. I drew the gable houses next to it (16). That's the first time I invented the context. I shifted the adjacent hip roofs to line up with mine. I've asked many students to invent sites. It's very important to learn to invent *from* the building, rather than to respond to the city. It's absolutely essential. In other words, you make the architecture that responds to the context by inverting the process and actually designing the circumstances that it responds to.

Picasso didn't intend to create monsters. He was looking for new forms with which to depict reality. Cornered House could almost be a part of the lexicon of suburban forms of houses, one that Venturi could possibly have accepted. It wasn't conspicuously avant-garde. It was trying to be normal, but barely. Of course, it's stretching the limits, but it has the picture window and a meandering sidewalk. That sidewalk, by the way, zigzagged up into the house and became an oblique plane that passed through the building and then shaved off the head house of the staircase from the garage below (17). Talking about succession! All of a sudden, the ground is tipped up to become a ramped plane that slices the facade and interior of the house.

BALLIET: We talked about the early houses in connection to many of the later projects, many of which start to engage the plazas or rise up in different ways.

COHEN: They do, you're absolutely right. All of these houses were all about getting above the ground. It's like the piloti with Villa Savoye. It's about relinquishing the ground plane to the city. In terms of succession, the key in all three houses—Longboat Key, Siesta Key, and Cornered House—is the Palladian problem that I talked about with the grand stair going up. Architecture has always been about going *up*, one way or another, whether upon a pedestal or in such a way that the ground floor is evacuated. Even this building, Knowlton Hall, is kind of evacuated on the first floor. Longboat Key is lifted because there was a floodplain and because I wanted the plan to do something it couldn't

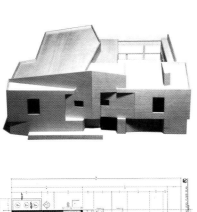

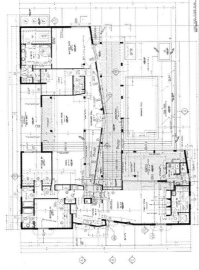

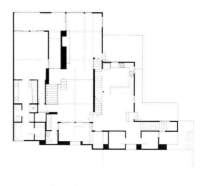

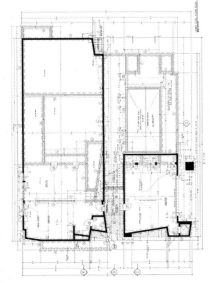

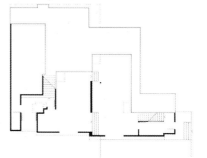

11 House on Longboat Key, Preston Scott Cohen,1985-87

12 House on Siesta Key, Preston Scott Cohen, 1989

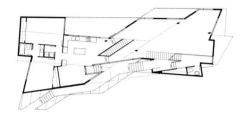

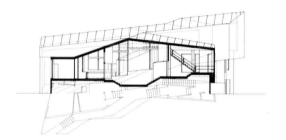

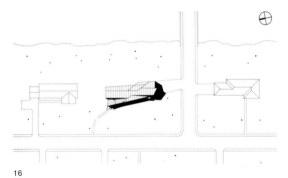

16

13 Cornered House, Preston Scott Cohen, 1990-91

14 Amir Building, Tel Aviv Museum of Art, Preston Scott Cohen, 2003-11

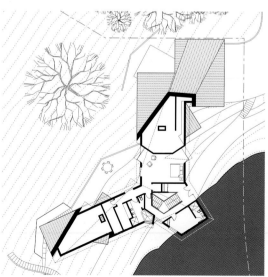

15 Fahmy House, Preston Scott Cohen, 2007, 2016

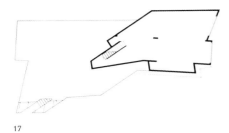

17

15 Fahmy House, Preston Scott Cohen, 2007, 2016

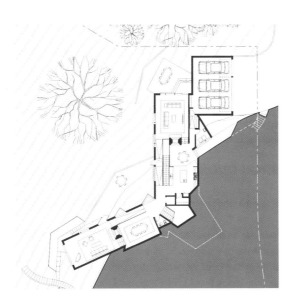

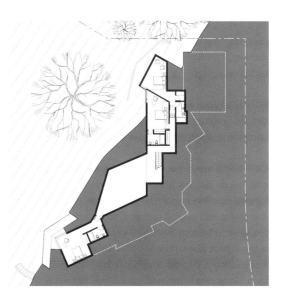

otherwise do. I wanted the occupant to enter at the center. I'm obsessed with this kind of sequence. I'm sure you all noticed the spiral. The spiral is already implicit in the sequence of Longboat.

BALLIET: I'm interested in the Torus House (18) and how it terminates into the ground. It has the core spatial element and it deals with the five points in a different way. It deals with the issue of pure geometry. It might be good to discuss this house in reference to some of these other issues we have put on the table. I know we had some questions come up when the students and I were discussing that project. For example, why the torus? Why that particular geometry? Was it arbitrary? We had a relative split between those who thought it was arbitrary and those who though it was a pretty intelligent selection of a particular geometry to solve a problem, even though it was a problem you made up yourself. It was a project that brought up a lot of interesting discussion points.

STUDENT: In terms of formmaking, how do you choose a certain problem? For example, how did you decide to introduce the torus into that project? How do you know what problems to address?

COHEN: Aargh! (Class laughs) That's a hard question to answer … it's irksome. God, I don't know. We talk about it all the time in the office. This is a torturous issue. We always know why we do it. We just know that it's good to do it. I don't know how to explain it. But then we move away from the starting point. We almost always lose the starting point with every project. That's really important, by the way.

STUDENT: But even if it was just an investigation, what did you get out of the Torus House that led you to continue pushing these issues?

COHEN: It made me realize that an abstract form could become an allegory of an architectural anomaly. The toroidal opening through which the stair passes on its way to the roof is both too small to be a courtyard and too large to be simply a stair well. The whole Torus House is like a thick wall with a window rotated horizontally so that you move through it vertically (19). Meanwhile, the form categorically cancels the discreet definition of things. It melds everything to create a new version of

ambiguity. Floor, wall and ceiling become unified. I wanted to make the whole into a single thing (20).

Presently, I am fascinated by the opposite—which is how to make architecture out of all of its parts. I'm interested in architecture that is absolutely impossible to bring together. I don't want to smooth it out and make it all one thing because I know it isn't. I'm not going to pretend anymore. In fact, I want to make more evident the fact that it is inherently disintegrated.

STUDENT: Le Corbusier claimed that architecture exists when a window is too small or too big. It seems like you have an obsession with difference. Are you interested in creating architecture that expresses difference? In the Eyebeam Competition (21), why did you insert these geometric shapes to hold up the structure?

BALLIET: You have also said that it's a collection of active architectural elements. Are you interested in peculiar combinations? Because I think all of those things set up a certain demand for attention. Or a wrestling match, maybe?

COHEN: The Eyebeam proposal represents a concept I called "Toroidal Architecture." It is composed of spaces turned inside out. Intersecting cones and cylinders generate spatial voids containing escalators and beams held in compression by a structural system of tensegrity, similar to and inspired by the sculptures of Kenneth Snelson. The combination of the linear elements of the tensegrity system and the geometric surfaces produce a dualistic space of interlocked toruses. The toruses of Eyebeam come from the Torus House and the Wu House; the linear elements and surfaces, which serve as an organizational diagram for a museum space, were the inspiration for the Tel Aviv Museum Lightfall (22).

PROJECTION

People in the schools tend to think that the projective drawings (23) were the most interesting thing that I was working on at the beginning. Yet, I regard the intricate drawings of those years, in and of themselves, to be a project that became myopic. I would also like to acknowledge that it's very important for the architect to digress and occasionally to set aside the larger mission.

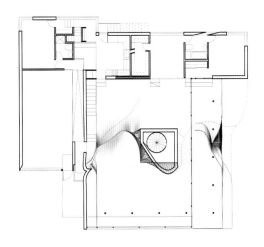

19

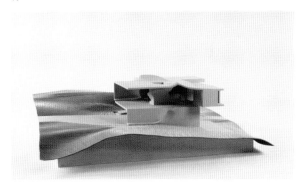

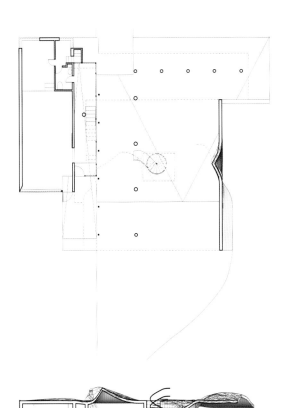

18

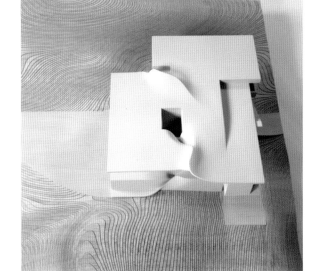

20 Torus House, Preston Scott Cohen, 1999

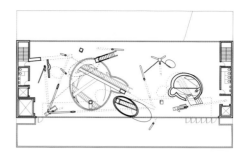

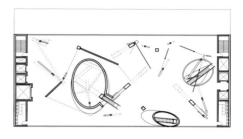

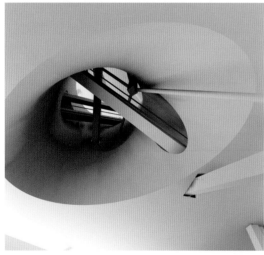

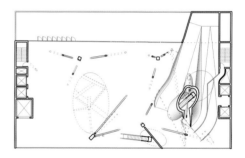

21 Eyebeam Atelier Museum, Preston Scott Cohen and Cameron Wu, 2001

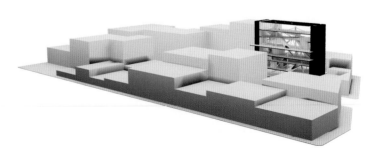

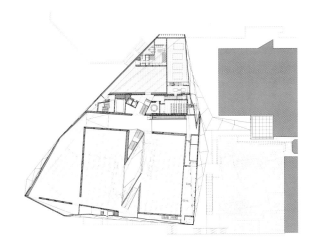

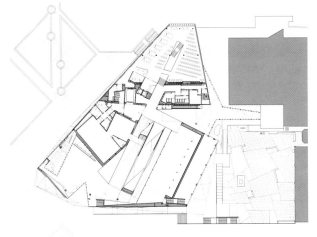

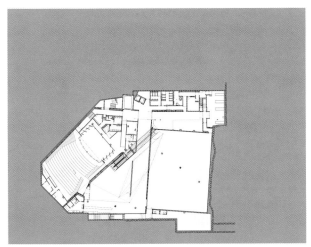

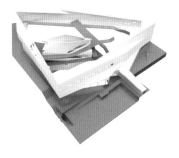

22 Amir Building, Tel Aviv Museum of Art, Preston Scott Cohen, 2003-11

After all, the focus on projective geometry did ultimately contribute in significant ways to Tel Aviv Museum, Taiyuan Museum, the Goldman Sachs canopy (24), Datong Library (25), and Keystone School (26).

The projective drawings were about the idea of distortion, an idea that remains operative in the projects I'm doing today. The idea of projecting something onto an oblique plane that results in an anamorphic depiction of a true (normally projected) image is a fascinating thing. You end up with a distorted, attenuated representation. The idea of attenuation—I'll never *not* be interested in. It presents something that you don't see normally. If I'm putting something in your peripheral vision that is normally right in front of your eyes, I am turning peripheral vision into central vision. Architecture does that because it's always an exception to the ordinarily built environment and to normative culture. Architecture tries to stand apart. Distortion is a very literal way to make something evidently different from the normal. Moreover, it's very compelling to me because it goes to the heart of how we construct the image of architecture with perspective. It goes to the heart of how we make architecture through orthographic projection and how we model it. This is a spatial idea. It's about projecting something through space and thinking about it as being transmitted and transformed. To move from that idea into another three-dimensional reality sounds wonderful. It's a great idea to think about.

BALLIET: One of the very first texts on those early explorations was Weinstock's review of you. He recognizes two projects happening: the drawing and geometric are one of the projects while the other is about drawing as a means of form making.

COHEN: Drawing as the basis of architecture is very problematic. First, let me indict drawing for some of its most heinous crimes. For one, it was the source of cartoonish postmodernism. What Graves did was to turn architecture into a representational drawing (27). He attempted to make buildings look like his drawings. There were no tectonic considerations, just drywall. There was no interrelationship of space and cladding to structure. There was no necessary relationship between the proportion of things and the structure. Yet, as we know, structure is a determining and necessary agent and—after staircases, circulation, and the plan—is

probably the strongest and most convincingly authoritative source for architectural form. The beauty of his drawings is that they gave only an impression of architecture. When he actually tried to build the impression, he destroyed it.

The Deconstructivists turned architecture into graphic design. They translated two-dimensional lines into sticks and planes. The sticks (beams and columns) of their projects were originally lines on a piece of paper. You could say that their process was an attempt to reinvent the language of architecture. Someone could argue that they expanded the repertoire by making a structure out of all of these sticks. But the sticks did nothing other than hold themselves up. They were rhetorical with nothing to say.

When I became chair at the GSD I wanted to get rid of the required drawing course. Everyone was in a state of shock. They just didn't follow my thinking. But anyone who knew me could understand how I had arrived at that position. Moreover, with computer modeling, you don't need to do hand projection. You can turn your attention immediately to geometry and to architectural typologies and tectonics.

I enjoy the pressure that geometry puts on us. It is absolutely beautiful. The only thing that was really important about the projective drawings—leaving aside whether or not I like the projects that arose from them—was that projection provided a force of law and a reason for the form. The lack of reasons, a problem that architecture had arrived to, weighed on me and continues to do so. Projection Architecture was once regulated by a canon. You could not do *this* with the window without it being out of proportion. You could not do *this* with entablatures and do *that* with columns. The canonic laws of architecture regulated the proportionality of architecture. These laws necessitated it by and through previously-originating theories. After the modern period, we are left with *anything goes*, formally speaking. The form of architecture became unintellectual, unguided, and without purpose.

Functionality is insufficient to determine the precise shape and composition of architecture. I can say I need light to be somewhere. But I could do the mullions a little differently and there are many types of windows I could use. There is not a precise fit between function and form that could ever be pictorially sufficient to relieve you of the burden of the *anything goes* of

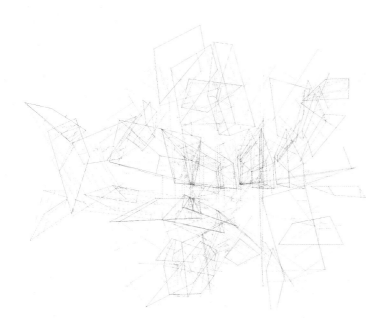

23 Projective Geometry, Head Start Competition, Preston Scott Cohen, 1994

24 Goldman Sachs Canopy, Preston Scott Cohen, 2005-09

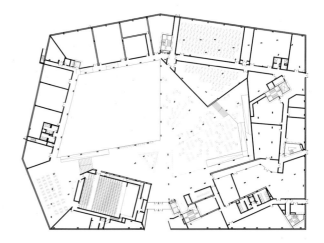

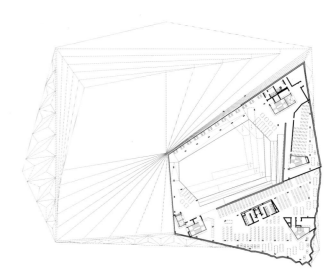

25 Datong Library, Preston Scott Cohen, 2008-14

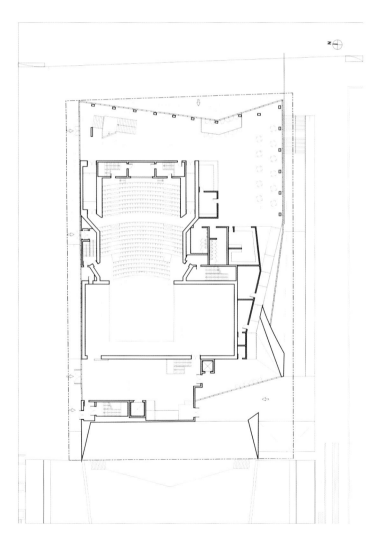

26 Keystone Academy Performing Arts Center, Preston Scott Cohen, 2011-15

architecture. I hate this ultimate and absolute freedom. One needs to have a dialectic and a constraint of form.

Why is architecture a social practice? It is authored to such great extent by so many things other than ourselves. It is authored through a long history of construction. It is authored through function and habits that produced the rules that many have written before us. It's like language. Architecture is about confronting extrapersonal matters. I dislike loose and purely willful shapemaking in architecture. My work has been about trying to get past this, but without resorting to the usual processes of practice and without having a unified, conventional language of architecture. We don't have a shared language to speak of and so we all are making our own noises as architects. This is not a good situation to be in.

Both Alberti and Wright—looking at two people from two very different periods—condemned perspective and called it illusory and untruthful. Wright was a great perspectivist and Alberti was a theorist of painting. Both refused to include perspective in the discipline of architecture. Although there is a lot of perspective that is very important to Alberti, he doesn't think that you produce architecture by imagining it pictorially. Architecture is a collective endeavor that is built upon a shared base condition from which to communicate our place in the world. You can't do that with personal expression, which is about yourself. Architecture does not arise from artists or painters who are trying to represent their inner feelings.

Drawing is not architecture. Drawing is not a substitute for architecture. I think people in schools tend to imbue drawing with undue authority and poeticism because they don't know how to think architecturally. It's too hard to teach architecture. It is too difficult to make architecture interesting. Drawing is something that can be taught much more easily. The problem for me is that I am interested in architecture, not drawing.

SUCCESSIVE ARCHITECTURE

Something else happened during the period in which drawing, personal expression, and postmodernism dominated: the city became architecture. Architecture was thought to be a direct product of the city, as if the two were one. This premise is deceptive and has led to misunderstandings. In fact, quite the opposite is true;

architecture is a decidedly different species of space and culture than the city. Architecture doesn't succumb to the spatial logic of urbanization; it is forced by the city to be different. Only single-story buildings and freestanding houses can be considered isomorphic with sprawl. All other buildings are destined to contend with something that only architecture, as opposed to urbanization, deals with: the stacking of space within discreet parcels.

After the elevator and the accessibility requirements became universal, spatial piling became endemic to buildings tall and short alike. I have named "Successive Architecture" the buildings that either intensify or countermand the salient problematic traits of vertical spatial stacking. And what are these?

First of all, the ground floor is self-contradictory; it is both part of the stack and not, at once (28) unified with the city or suburb and part of the series. Unlike any other space in the stack, its threshold is not beholden to the elevator and it is not necessarily limited by the facade.

The ascendency from bottom to top, which implies successive stacking (one floor after another) is contradicted by the static simultaneity of the non-hierarchical repetition of stories. Also extremely important, obviously, is the disparity between the spatial multiplicity of the inside and the singularity of the outside.

The freestanding house, a constituent of urban sprawl that is not obligated to be constituted as a stack and is thus not inherently architectural, can be converted into architecture, nonetheless. Mies's Farnsworth House is like one story cut from a skyscraper (29). He, Wright, Johnson, and others volunteered to make houses imitate the fundamental spatial and tectonic characteristics of stacking that the city mandates only occur in larger, multi-story buildings.

Venturi went further and did something hilarious in this regard. He didn't explicitly say that the suburban house isn't architecture, but he must have thought so because he insisted on making houses that looked like institutional buildings. First, let's back up and note that the Vanna Venturi house (30), presumably a manifestation of his empathy with the common man, is actually a sophisticated interpretation of Le Corbusier. It doesn't look like an American suburban house at all. It's planar and super abstract. Yes, it has a gable form but it doesn't have overhangs and is—tectonically—unmistakably atypical.

Later he produces the Brant House (31), a private house in Connecticut, the facade of which is made of green glazed brick. Glazed brick was then a common material for

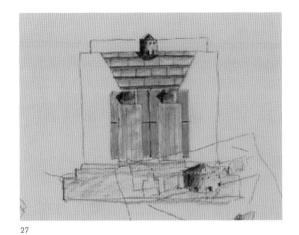

27

29

30

31

28

schools and certain kinds of commercial buildings, hospitals, etcetera. It was part of the vernacular landscape. His desire for ornament is fulfilled by him introducing patterns that are normally found in the brick that you see on these commercial buildings.

The Dream House (32)—ironically—is just a box. He finally decides to make a house an *actual* decorated shed. It doesn't have any pushes or pulls. It doesn't have any engagement with the site: no bay windows, nothing. Here is a country house that should be in the city. Why was he making a country house this way? Basically, he's just making a purely theoretical project. The one typology that does not need to be a decorated shed is the freestanding house. Thus, he is needlessly making a house into a decorated shed. Traditionally, the house never had a conflict between the inside and the outside. Look at a Victorian house. A Victorian house has explosions of irregular bay windows and idiosyncratic breakages of symmetry. It is a type of house that is free of the laws of the classical. It is free to be engaged and directly expressive of need in all the ways we'd want it to be. There is no need to force it into this horrible problem that buildings have, which is that they have skins and are filled with horizontal slabs. For buildings, there's no natural relationship between the inside and the outside. With Dream House, he makes a house this way. He's volunteering to draw the house back into the realm of architecture. He's forcing it to be architecture by destroying the essence of what a house really is. He is substituting the beautiful complexity and contradiction inherent to houses with really ugly patterns of shiny brick and with windows that are too big and too small. It's a brilliant theoretical commentary on the problem of the house. It's about the idea of houses versus buildings.

Le Corbusier made houses that look like buildings too. All of the houses with ribbon windows could become skyscrapers. The Villa Savoye (33) is successive architecture. It just happens to be only three stories. The middle story of Villa Savoye could easily be propagated. For Le Corbusier, there is no house. Everything is architecture: a building by virtue of successivity. By introducing a giant, open elevator, Koolhaas verified that the Corbusian house was a very short skyscraper (34).

PLEASANT STREET BUILDING

This project, the transformation of a small warehouse into my office, summarizes many things. The project is one of a series of projects that deal with typological readymades. Perhaps more importantly, it is one of several projects for which reflected light is a significant protagonist. Let me begin by saying that what I found so imminently pleasant about this building was the way in which it availed itself to concepts of successive architecture.

The building is directional with an unmistakable front (35). Originally, it was a glass-fronted grocery store and a tube space was extruded away from Pleasant Street. In the 1960s it was converted into a floor tile warehouse and the facade was infilled with white glazed brick of the sort that Venturi likes. A loading door was inserted on the Laurel Street side in a very lewd, crude way. The door was hacked out in an asymmetrical location (36) irrespective of the side elevation's two large symmetrically disposed brick frames.

Having two doors permitted me to bring about an implied 90-degree rotation of the plan (37, 38). Whereas the original front door is centered on the existing steel structural beam and a row of columns that bisects the main space, the side-loading door is now centered on a new 36' long skylight that stretches the length of the space. On the interior, the well of the skylight and the southern light it reflects on the northern wall—the "77 Pleasant Street Lightfall"—makes the side facade more important than the old front (39).

The plan, rotated 90 degrees, now has two fronts, a duality that is not dictated by the logic and the morphology given to the building by the city. Re-orientation, displacement, and its consequences are related to the simultaneity and flicker effect of architectural anamorphosis and the toroidal centrifugal plans of many other projects such as Goodman and Torus House. More importantly, in this case they imply a z-axis that denies the x and y (the front and side orientations of the original building, respectively) any definitive hierarchy. The introduction of non-orientation, whereby the y-axis becomes as significant as the x, equalizes the points of entry along the perimeter. The fact that the space is top-lit like a gallery and is inward facing in order to maximize privacy and inconspicuousness, makes the interior the primary definer of the building's orientation.

The side door, having been positioned off center, pulls the skylight along with it, away from the back of the building and, in doing so, also accommodates the new apartment. A new wall, angled to both accept the length of the skylight in the main space and to accommodate the widest part of

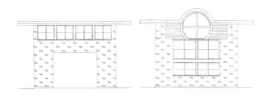

34

32

33

35 Pleasant Street Gallery and Studio, Preston Scott Cohen, 2012-13

the apartment behind, also centers a small, previously inserted skylight that otherwise had no relationship to the building as a whole. That skylight had been added when the building was partitioned during its most recent use as a warehouse.

I introduced two new steel beams to support the roof that flank the new skylight well (40). These beams rest upon the principle steel beam that acts as a spine running down the center of the space which in turn rests upon a steel beam that spans across the formerly glass storefront. With the addition of the new beams, the roof structure becomes triply, successively stacked.

Because the skylight produces reflected southern light, when the door in the north wall is open, the color temperature of the interior is not discernibly different than the light falling on the house across the street. As a result, interior and exterior merge. Seen from Pleasant Street through the windows on the front facade, the reflected southern light with shadows of the beams cast on the interior wall, makes the building look roofless. The shadows seem to belong to the electrical street wires. As another sign of successive architecture, this effect of *emptying out* suggests that the facades are a manifestation of vertical extrusion rather than surfaces enclosing a volume.

The basement is populated by irregularly-distributed columns. It is as if it is the ground level space of a building on pilotis was displaced downward until the floor of the main space is precisely coincident with the street. This coincidence, in turn, contributes to the seamless continuity with the outdoors.

When one enters the building, it appears to be a single room, an extreme case of isomorphism between the inside and the outside. In fact, this is an illusion. The newly added angled rear wall acts as a party wall between the main space and the apartment. During construction, I decided to pivot the wall in order to provide a window on the south facade of the building to the apartment. Note that in the basement the angled wall remains in its original position, allowing the vertically compressed basement space to expand horizontally in an indiscernible way.

The apartment is raised a few steps. The window looks out onto the neighbor's slightly raised rear yard garden. This bucolic setting contrasts with the view through the interior window of the angled party wall that looks out over the entire main space which, when

naturally top lit, seems as if it is an enclosed courtyard. The patched floor recalls a parceled hardscape between disparate surrounding urban buildings.

It would be possible to imagine a linear sequence that begins with the stair rising from the basement— flanking wall and skylight overhead—and continues into the apartment and up the apartment's stair, which also passes directly underneath a linear skylight running along the party wall. This sequence begins on the fictional ground level and concludes at the window to the garden. In this sense, the building pays homage to Villa Savoye. The other precedents for the building, according to Rafael Moneo, are the small banks of Louis Sullivan (41), the father of one very important solution for successive architecture as told in "The Tall Building Artistically Considered."

36

39

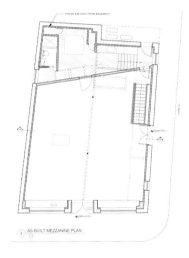

37 AS-BUILT MEZZANINE PLAN

40

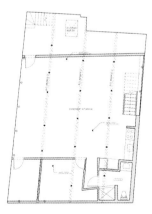

38 AS-BUILT BASEMENT PLAN

41

ANALYSIS AND COMMENTARY

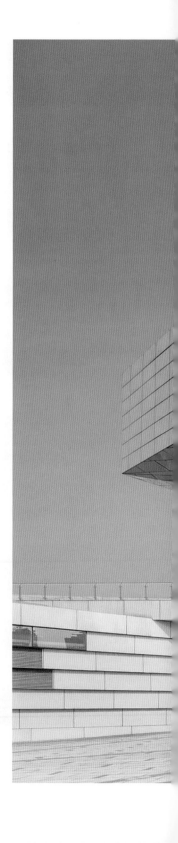

The Expanded Interior

Kristy Balliet

The expanded interior exceeds the volume that is designated to contain it. It goes beyond the limits of physical scale. The expanded interior relies on perception and engages visual connections with other adjacent volumes, both interior and exterior. It is a volumetric outpouring unbound by architecture alone. The expanded interior contorts in order to test the limits of enclosure. It is motivated to connect beyond limits; it is an architectural stretch.

The work of Preston Scott Cohen encompasses these ambitions in the form of predicaments. Predicaments, even if fabricated, sponsor innovation. While many architects today seek to shrink the scale of architecture, Cohen swallows the 'bigness' of architecture. He has consistently invested in the exploration of inner worlds, hidden cores, and internal vastness—less in terms of scale and more in terms of impact—using complex volumes. Having developed design expertise throughout his career, Cohen focuses on the expanded interior.

Each project curates containment in order to sponsor the will for expansion. The development of this productive tension matters. Tension is not dependent on scale or monumental gestures; it is fashioned at the margins and it trades in degrees rather than grandeur. It is found in the nuances and can be anywhere. This tension manifests itself in a variety of ways within architectural proposals, and in Cohen's work it embodies a constant moving from the status quo toward the precise design of new problems. This attention is significant in a discipline that increasingly sees its primary role as solving problems rather than creating them. To have a project that seeks to expand the interior is indeed an alternative mode of contemporary operation. The design emphasis of the expanded interior implies multiple alternatives for architecture and its interiors, exteriors, and connective urban realms.

The expanded interior fights containment. By most definitions, buildings contain many rooms. These rooms negotiate for positions. Consider the arrangement of rooms in Palladio's Villa Rotunda or, at the urban scale, Soane's Bank of England: as the assembly of interior volumes or rooms increases so do typological complexities. In many cases, buildings contain more than one building. The rooms and their perimeters negotiate their relationship to one another. Minimal differences exist between interior and exterior movement, extending the immersive experience. These struggles—or as Cohen refers to them, *predicaments* and *contested situations*—require the development of precise qualities and robust spatial ambitions in order to engage and sustain attention. The larger project is the curated struggle between these conditions, and the result is the proliferation and design of thresholds or interstitial spaces.

Preston Scott Cohen manifests the expanded interior in two major ways. First, Cohen pulls exteriors through (or into) the interiors. He absorbs courtyards, displaces interior space, and twirls centers into their own project. The second tactic modifies containment using multiples. Multiplication can include instances such as split roof ridges, congruent barrel vaults, and the coupling of programs. In both cases, the work of Cohen expands circulatory volume, bloats issues of entry, and strains formal relationships.

When the exterior maneuvers to fill the interior, subtle (or not so subtle) torques, folds, and creases emerge. The projects oscillate when agitated, turning outside in or inside out, and expand beyond their expected limits. Many of Cohen's early houses exhibit this character (1, 2) and it is a trait that remains present through more recent projects such as the Tel Aviv Museum of Art.

In each of these examples, exteriors are captured as interiors. Geometric vortices torque surfaces and reorient views and occupation. There is an abrupt discovery that the space at the center is exterior (3).

In many of the projects the user never occupies the center because the sequence of circulation moves around the perimeter. The early houses introduce problems with geometrical consequences that expose internal contradictions. Normative qualities such as domestic necessity are challenged and new typologies evolve.[1] Cohen states that, "The struggle to preserve the idea of the torus, then, produces a rather peculiar house. Of course there is no reason why a house must evoke the idea of the torus. But without it, there would be no problem at all."[2] Instead of keeping the anomaly on the fringe, Cohen places the normative and the anomaly in the same weight class and a contest ensues.

1 Torus House, Preston Scott Cohen, 1999

This type of contest is best exhibited in the Fahmy House, a design for a severe hillside site in Los Gatos, California. The V-shaped plan kinks to draw the exterior deep within. The interior gathers around this moment and expands the entry sequence to either side, forming a swollen bowtie. The connective foyers and circulation cores grow beyond their normative role and exploit the vertical and horizontal spatial strength that these elements have within the domestic realm (4). In a description of the Fahmy House, Cohen explains that interior space is exceeding the volume. He states, "volumes can be effectively (speaking in architectural terms) exceeded by spaces 'leaking out' of them if the volumes are clearly defined on their own terms."[3] Volumes are reshaped and can be defined, modeled, and built to transcend a compilation of single rooms. They can have names in their own right and are selective in commanding adjacencies. They are puzzles without borders.

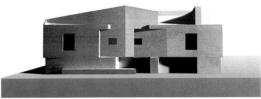

2 House on Longboat Key, Preston Scott Cohen, 1985-87

The second tactic of the expanded interior engages multiples. It is perhaps best shown by way of Cohen's *Lightfall*, the most exemplary of the expanded interiors in which volume performs. The project itself is sited within the larger project of the Tel Aviv Museum of Art (5). Together, the two projects redefine architectural containment. *Lightfall* (while technically within the museum) cannot be considered a contained central volume because the *Lightfall* can stand alone. And it does (6). This expanded interior mimics the exterior and has been the subject of solo exhibitions, has been included in larger exhibitions (11th Venice Biennale as a scale model), and is the subject of a forthcoming book, entitled *Lightfall*.[4] The project, first

3 Goodman House, Preston Scott Cohen, 2001-04

4 Fahmy House, Preston Scott Cohen, 2007, 2016

represented as a complete interior, continues to define the Tel Aviv Museum of Art today. Cohen describes the building as, "initially composed of four rooms on three floors" and a coupling of a museum and a library.[5] The two buildings bound by a single envelope vie for a direct relationship to the exterior, and in doing so they expand their respective interiors.

Redefining the container is prevalent in much of Cohen's later work. In most cases, multiple buildings are assembled within a range of various 'wrapper' tactics. The Taiyuan Museum of Art—the subject of this book—expands the previous rules for building-and-wrapper relationships, but the contest remains. Taiyuan is no longer a single building trying to contain multiple buildings, but is rather a cluster of buildings contained by promenades (7, 8). Here, the role of the enclosure extends beyond the building shell to engage courtyards, circulation, and fractured entries. There is a constant play of catch and release. Unlike in Tel Aviv, where two buildings wrestle into one, Taiyuan exposes the multiplicity and generates outdoor rooms and pockets: a contemporary Unity Temple. There is a surge of corners, niches, and layered cornices or the architectural equivalent of James Turrell's 'skyspaces.'[6] In each of these instances, the design of the relationship between the interior and perimeter exceeds expectation and challenges a common desire for rooms and buildings to logically resolve their collective and individual relationships with the exterior. The selection of terms used to describe the plurality of interiors changes with each project (*clusters*, *hybrids*), but the interest in setting up a contest between singles and multiples remains throughout.

In order for architecture to be endowed with the ambition to expand its interior, it requires a co-dependent relationship with the designed struggle for containment. The container must be designed to produce multiple interiors, and architectural space needs to become more inclusive of both interiors and exteriors. Cohen has mastered and exploited the techniques of capturing volume with tactics that range from a bear hug—accommodating existing terrain or buildings with outstretched arms—to the headlock, a stuffed infilling. These and others set up conditions meant to secure subtle variations between the interior and exterior and that have evolved to challenge architectural relationships. The result is a series of projects that manifest the idiomatic expression, "say 'uncle,'" although we are not really ready to be freed from the architectural 'knot' yet.[7]

Notes

1. Preston Scott Cohen, "Torus House," in Contested Symmetries and Other Predicaments in Architecture, 2004. Princeton Architectural Press, NY, p138. 'The synthesis of normative features (floors, stairs) with a curvilinear element implicitly unifies a singular form alien to architecture – the torus – with several historically pervasive architectural types – the courtyard, the stairwell, the lightwell.'

2. Preston Scott Cohen, "Predicaments and Surrogates," in Contested Symmetries and Other Predicaments in Architecture, 2004. Princeton Architectural Press, NY, p12–15.

3. Excerpt from Scott Cohen's e-mail response to a student inquiry, dated November 11, 2014: 'There, the interior space most obviously descends within the volume and proceeds to descend obliquely under that point into a space under the sloped ground plane, thus exceeding the volume. I hope this helps you to understand. When we spoke, I speculated that volumes can be effectively (speaking in architectural terms) exceeded by spaces "leaking out" of them if the volumes are clearly defined on their own terms.'

4. Lightfall: Genealogy of a Museum: Paul and Herta Amir Building, Tel Aviv Museum of Art. (New York: Skira, expected October 2016).

5. Preston Scott Cohen lecture notes, dated November 3, 2014.

6. A Turrell Skyspace is a specifically proportioned chamber with an aperture in the ceiling open to the sky. Skyspaces can be autonomous structures or integrated into existing architecture. The aperture can be round, ovular, or square. http://jamesturrell.com/work/type/skyspace/

7. Preston Scott Cohen, 'The Inevitable Flatness of Floors Interests Me,' in Log 28 'Stocktaking,' Guest edited by Peter Eisenman and Anthony Vidler, Summer 2013.

5 Amir Building, Tel Aviv Museum of Art, Preston Scott Cohen, 2003-11

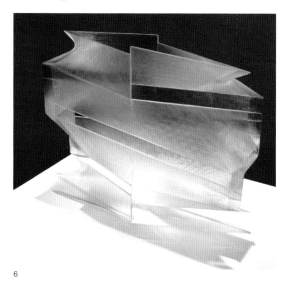
6

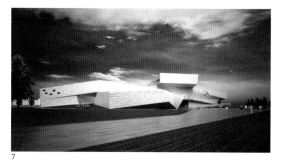
7

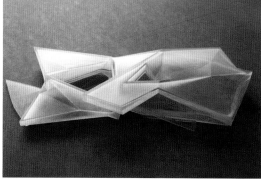
8 Taiyuan Museum of Art, Preston Scott Cohen, 2007-13

A Maze on Domino

Doug Graf

THE PROGRAM

The Taiyuan Art Museum immediately suggests something both familiar and unfamiliar. For one thing, the art museum program seems clear enough, but few of us could locate Taiyuan on a map or provide any other information about it, other than confusing it with Taiwan. And what is the cause of this newly expressed need? We are aware that art museums are being built all over China, but to hold what? Does the art exist now, and, if so, where? Or have the museums been designed for future art or a future collection that is currently non-existent? Or is the demand not for museums for art, but the museums themselves? Given the trajectory of the role of the art museum over the last several centuries, the answer may be the latter.

In the Western world, the audience for art has evolved slowly over time to include ever-larger numbers of people. Originally comprised of visiting aristocracy and connoisseurs, the visitors came to include newly rich industrialists, middle-class professionals, the middle class in general, and finally the hordes associated with mass tourism. The English lord passing through Florence in the 18th century might not immediately recognize his connection to his halter-topped, pram-pushing equivalent in the 21st century, but they are merely the two ends of a continuous trajectory.

Probably for a number of reasons, an era that spends substantially less on art on a per capita basis than in previous centuries has also spawned a population that dotes on art museums. Part of the explanation for this situation can likely be traced back to the great exhibitions of the 19th century. Art became one of the great attractors, on equal footing with topics such as Industry, Agriculture, Transportation, and others that, in contrast, currently hold a far diminished allure for us. In the United States, a number of significant art collections owe their existence to these exhibitions: the Philadelphia Museum of Art was organized in 1876 to provide material for the Centennial Exhibition of that year, the Chicago Art Institute had a similar connection to the Columbian Exposition of 1893, the St. Louis museum was a consequence of the 1904 World's Fair, and San Francisco's Legion of Honor was built as a consequence of the Panama Pacific Exposition of 1915. During this century of exploration, discovery, and colonialism, the focus of the exhibitions increasingly began to include interests that were more exotic and/or ethnographic in nature, such as model dinosaurs, the art and architecture of exotic people, and eventually the exotic people themselves, preferably scantily clad. Eventually, a visit to the exhibitions and world's fairs became more than an opportunity for edification and education. These events became an opportunity for amusement and diversion in which the latest art would segue into the latest locomotive, the latest fast food, the latest three-legged cow, and possibly a bit of hoochie coochie and a few thrill rides.

An attempt was made to separate Art from this mélange by reintroducing it into distinctive institution differentiated by both architecture and site. The presence of such an institution within the city had the benefit of giving a civic boost to the aspirations of these various boomtowns that had grown out of the wilderness and sought recognition on the urban stage. Not unlike contemporary China, vast new museums began to appear in places where only buffalo and fur traders could be found a century or less earlier, places like ... well, Buffalo, as well as Cleveland, Detroit, Chicago, St. Louis, Kansas City, San Francisco, and countless others. The impulse was much like the Middle Ages, when cities strove to boost their status by promoting their connection to the local saint (even if it meant stealing the body of someone else's), and is comparable to the contemporary American desire to be graced with a professional sports team (even if Tampa's connection to ice hockey is no more strained than Venice's to St. Mark).

Inevitably, these buildings were constructed in a style that was both recognizable and sanctioned by the era, but also understood as institutional and distinct. Such codification permitted them to be separated from the rough and tumble everyday urban landscape that characterized most of these cities. Viewing art meant one was absorbed in a special activity—Culture— as opposed those activities of the common urban experience. Especially in the United States, the location of the museum itself sought separation from the crassness of the everyday, by seeking refuge and the sanitized isolation of the new landscape parks that were being constructed in virtually every city.

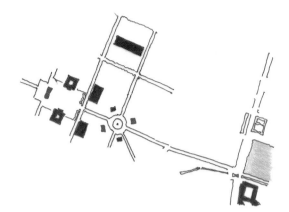

Although the museums were new, the basic models were not. They were the museums of Europe, which, if not actually located within an existing palace, were also relatively recent newcomers, many built in the first half of the 19th century. They were largely the result of royal collections being given to the public, often to placate the middle class and perhaps to divert them from ideas about democracy. Munich is a particularly interesting example, and somewhat like America, in that a new district—organized in relationship to the spine of Briennerstrasse—was laid out to accommodate the new citadels of culture as a collection of pavilions distinct from the fabric of the existing city (1). In a spate of construction that might have been referred to as the 'Munich Effect,' the city was suddenly front and center in the art world, as Von Klenze provided the plans for the Glyptothek (1830) and also the Pinakothek (1836), which was at the time the largest art museum in the world.

Sometime between the Pinakothek and Bilbao, the art museum became a focus of mass visitation on a scale never seen before. A number of things were responsible: greater wealth, growth of the middle classes, the provision of cheap transportation, and the growth of mass tourism in general. But to some degree the change was encouraged by Modernism itself and its focus on providing forms derived from function rather than precedent. This opened opportunities for a much greater degree of novelty and experimentation, one result being that that the experience of the museum itself became as important as visiting its collections, if not more so. Although many of the museums of the 19th century were impressive, they tended to operate within a fairly narrow range of prescribed forms and features, especially compared with what was now appearing. But even within these proscriptive ranges, style emerged quickly as an important consideration.

In 1876, the Boston Museum of Fine Arts opened at a site on Copley Square in a Victorian Gothic building, but was replaced in 1909 by a Beaux Arts building on a different site, and the front facade of Calvert Vaux's original somewhat eclectic building for the Metropolitan Museum of 1880 was erased as the building was encased in Hunt's Beaux Arts addition of 1902, reflecting the stylistic stresses caused by the passage of between twenty-two to thirty-five years, respectively. Beaux Arts buildings remained the go-to solution for the major institutions throughout the first half of the 20th century (Buffalo-1905, Cleveland-1916, Philadelphia and Baltimore-1928, and Seattle-1933), but the next change was perhaps best marked by the difference between Pope's design for the National Gallery in Washington, which opened in 1941, and that for Wright's Guggenheim in New York, for which design began in 1943. Now, the museums were not just distinct from their surroundings, but distinct from anything.

These new buildings were capable of being stars in their own right, regardless of the quality of the collection or whether there was, in fact, a collection at all. The art museum increasingly began to appeal to people who not only weren't particularly interested in art, but also weren't previously interested in architecture, at least in terms of the prior manifestations. It was as though the relationship between the normative and the exotic that held sway during the 19th century was now reversed: what was previously a focus on the normative with a pinch of the exotic became primarily a focus on the exotic.

As exciting as the architecture of buildings such as the Taiyuan Art Museum is, it is also exceptional given the state of architecture across the rest of the city. This probably helps to solidify the continuing appeal of a city *museuming* itself. It provides a very different experience from the world of the everyday. Although Liebeskind's addition to the Denver Art Museum is accompanied by an attendant apartment building in compatible style, this has definitely not become the norm and would likely be self-defeating, as it would dilute the special status of the museum.

The situation in Taiyuan appears to mirror all the previous conditions: the strategy of the special landscape, the isolation of a cultural district, and the need to appeal to all sorts of people through a collection of the architecture of the exotic. In this case, discovering a collection of interestingly unusual buildings in a city made mostly from anything but interesting buildings is itself not particularly strange. There are similar situations all over China and, for that matter, the rest of the world. What might be unexpected given the taste for the exotic and the carte blanche to provide it is that three of the five buildings in the Taiyuan arts district have similar strategies in terms of exterior facades. They are all, more or less, creased, continuous surfaces. Perhaps this is the lingua franca of the era, as was the Beaux Arts in a previous time.

The efforts then are similar to the efforts now in that this style was understood to indicate a building of some significance that was, to a degree, distinct. The style couldn't guarantee the quality of the product and had little to do with the sophistication of any number of things: the plan, the quality of the spaces, the accommodation of the program, the usefulness of the circulation (whether for clarity, narrative, or surprise), etc. The results were unsurprisingly mixed, since they could be used skillfully or not to produce mundane, immediately surprising, quietly surprising, surprisingly mundane, or quietly mundane results. The range of successes can be seen if one were to compare the relative Classicism of Kent's Chiswick in London, Kengo Kuma's M2 Building in Tokyo (2, 3), or anything at Falwell's Liberty University, wherever the heck that is. In a trajectory that might illustrate the opportunities and problems offered by uninspected stylistic affections, the bold but assured experimentation with received norms of the first example evolves into the cacaphonic hilarity of the second, and then enters the land of the dead motifs exemplified by the last.

We can trace the history of architecture styles of the late 20th century by looking at many college campuses. The explosion of new construction in the decades that followed World War II might allow us to easily identify styles, but those styles won't be a guarantor of quality or competence even if, at the time, the construction of the buildings was felt to hold that promise. Certain stylistic impulses like Brutalism have often become the focus of the opposite impulse—an across the board revulsion, which is equally unjust. One might suspect that folded surface buildings are not immune from this phenomenon, a potential fact that may eventually disappoint a percentage of students currently in design studios.

The qualities that make Cohen's work so interesting are less about the identification of the style and more about the sophistication of strategies, the complex riches within configurations, the myriad relationships and their arguments, and the synthetic integration of innumerable vignettes and diagrammatic fragments. Taiyuan is a particularly interesting example of this array of tools at work. It is not surprising that the building, although contemporary and particular, manifests architectural devices, themes, motifs, and strategies that exist within the larger world of architectural form and intent. Yet some of these connections and similarities may be surprising. There is more happening here beyond the immediate impression of a contemporary impulse.

THE SITE

Regarding the tendency in the 19th century to locate art museums 'in the garden,' the building wasn't just plopped there. In general, there were two basic strategies. In the first case, the building was located on a street that bounded the park. In these instances, the museum essentially occupied two positions, one facade providing a prestigious urban address within the city and perhaps a bit of a forecourt, while the others established the building's credentials as a pavilion in the landscape (New York, Chicago, Boston). A low-budget but inventive variation would be a building that presents the expansive forecourt as a suggestion for the existence of a larger landscape, but quickly reveals the landscape as, in fact, a fiction (Columbus). In the second case, the connection to the city is scorned in order to best isolate and insulate the museum in it's own landscape. In increasing degrees of isolation, these might be represented by the art museums in Cleveland, Kansas City, St. Louis, and finally the surprising isolation of the buildings in Cincinnati or San Francisco).

2

3

At Taiyuan, the situation is less clear. Rather than organize the site for one particular building, the complex consists of five cultural facilities which are isolated as pavilions, but similarly placed, juxtaposed to create a common boundary around the park, thus minimizing their particularities as objects (and programs) as they are promoted as a single spatial barrier. Thus, here the 'park side' strategy is rendered relatively ineffective as an organizer of the building. Much the same can be said for the opportunity to utilize the 'city side,' partly because of the separation of the buildings from the city by a canal, but primarily because of the indifference of the development of the adjacent city parcels to the plan which offer little to connect to. Furthermore, the site landscape diagram provided to the architects seems to be a slightly unhappy amalgamation of two completely opposing strategies. Old School planners must have formulated the large-scale symmetrical arrangement of the five buildings; it is a static and stolid arrangement that we can imagine appealed to various party bureaucracies but that can't begin to hold the gargantuan space the structures are trying to surround. Agoraphobia appears to be the go-to strategy of many modern Chinese redevelopment areas, possibly as an over-the-top antidote to the general crowdedness of the cities. Whatever the cause, to the degree it is readable, the plan forces unwanted hierarchical interest on the central building at the expense of the flanking structures.

Contrasting with the stodginess of the larger site plan is the more detailed landscape plan for the park itself. This plan is organized around a cryptic hexagon in which a rotated square is vaguely implied, with neither figure employed for any particular purpose nor particularly sympathetic to the 'Old School'configuration (4). The result is a strategy that undermines the supposed equivalence of the buildings by offering ridiculously varied connections to them. One suspects the motif might have been formulated by some young designers—certainly not Old School, and possibly educated in the West—and seems to have a derived kinship with OMA's redo of Almere (5), which itself seems reminiscent of the Eisenman/Graves scheme for refiguring Harlem (6), which itself might have been inspired by the graphics of El Lissitsky or the original plan for the square that accommodates Barcelona's Diagonale to the grid of the city (7).

In opposition to the larger plan, the particular geometries offered by the hexagonal landscape plan create a variety of differentiated connections to the five buildings. The response from each project is mostly tepid as they conjure up their own individual landscape strategies instead. All five largely ignore the general grouping of buildings nearby that genuflect to a larger axis that in turn seems to have no particular relationship to the city. Although the double bridges across the river recognize this axis as an ensemble, they ignore it individually and do not have a particular relationship to the more intimate aspects of the geometries that radiate from the particular landscape plan. It is a puzzling choice since these particular diagonal geometries seem potentially sympathetic to the curving bridges.

The overriding impulse seems to be one in which multiple organizations are superimposed in an attempt to create something that suggests either variety or complexity, but to no particular effect. In fact, this might be offered as a criticism of much of the architecture surrounding the park, although the particular devices invoked are different. The wrapped surface buildings in particular seem to return us to the theme of the familiar versus the unfamiliar in that they contrast the certainty of the singular nature of the envelope with the oddness of their particularities, which seem to work against the principle of unity by which the facade strategy seems determined. In Cohen's hands, this will become a useful condition.

THE BUILDING

As a consequence of this variety of inclinations displayed by the site plan, we are left with a variety of opposing but relatively unrelated strategies. This makes a thoughtful response to the mélange of gestures difficult, if not impossible. One of the defining characteristics of the exterior of the Taiyuan Art Museum is that it keeps its head down and its powder dry. The building responds to the determined incongruities of the site by minimizing its exterior articulation. Where the site is a cacophony of superimposed motifs, the building makes a virtue of vagueness, which is one of the potential benefits of the way the continuous surface of the facade is employed. The elevation is both indeterminate and minimal. The exterior is formed by a surface that seems determined to mask the extremes of differentiation that

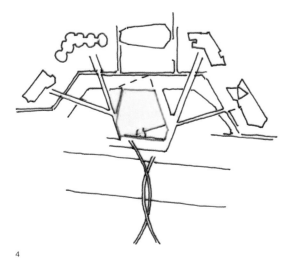

4

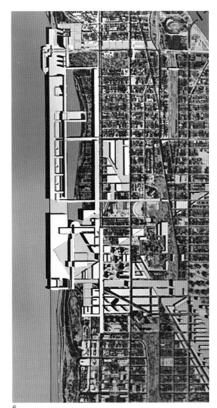

6

5

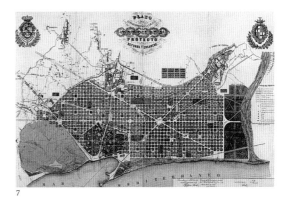

7

are occurring within and that are readily apparent under the wrapping. Stylistically the look is currently quite hip, but what is particularly useful about the organization is that it seems like a reasonable response to the difficulty of a thoughtful figural response to the site. The exterior is basically a cartoon that holds its place in the ensemble but is in a state of perpetual lack of completion. The building is almost literally 'under wraps,' although the interior is quite a different story.

It's interesting to contrast Taiyuan with Cohen's remarkable Tel Aviv Art Museum, a project with which there are strong elevational affinities. In Tel Aviv the building tends to be read as a single wrapper, but here the wraps and folds conspire to reformulate the relative chaos of the site and configure it into something much more urban and integral. The result is a series of new plazas that interlock at their corners, form connections and pathways, and create a new idea of the neighborhood structure while locking it all together (8). The scruffy inchoate character of the site is transformed into something more reminiscent of the spatial structure of cities, such as Salzburg's older core (9).

It's clear that Cohen not only has a fondness for the device of the ambiguously continuous surface but, more importantly, that he can use it to achieve very different results. In his hands it becomes an effective multipurpose tool rather than a look. It is interesting that although he has shown us it can be used to achieve a variety of ends, the strategy tends to be employed on larger projects rather than smaller. Cohen's Fahmy and Goodman residences use a diametrically opposed strategy in which the building is housed in a simple, familiar, and singular shape, regardless of the complexities on the interior (10, 11). As a consequence, an initial reaction when seeing the houses is that they have a slight retro sensibility, caught somewhere in a world between Newport and Chadds Ford (12). In this regard, one is perhaps reminded of a similar discrepancy of subject matter in the work of Charles Sheeler: farms versus factories, and the difference between domestic and the institutional and the suburb and the city.

This distinction reflects a possible difference in client attitudes regarding houses and museums: one desires the familiar and coherent while the other seeks the excitement of the unfamiliar and novel. With Cohen's work, what tends to link these two strategies is the fact

that, in either case, no particular emphasis is given to a specific three-dimensional component like a dormer, pavilion, appendage, or lump. Regardless of our initial sense that these are divergent architectures, the outer shells of his projects—whether house or museum or something entirely other—work to unify the building into a single argument.

In the case of Taiyuan, however, it's not as though there aren't specific readings of the building on the exterior. Within the continuous surface one detects a myriad of small discontinuities. The continuity of the surface, for example, is interrupted by the strong horizontality of the facades. This tends to reorganize the building in layers and these layers have a continuity of their own. To some degree, they imply the interior horizontal layering of the building that the exterior continuities seem to attempt to conceal, and similarly they can be read to suggest long bar-like tubes. As at Tel Aviv, although there is a general sense of formal amorphousness, there is also a contradictory reading of coherent—if incidental—orderliness, or even downright rectangularity, that differentiates areas within the surface of the building. In this case, the various components of the surface tend to be read as the tops, bottoms, or sides of the tubular substructures. For the most part, these tubes appear to continue across the facade and around the corners, a reading made easier by the non-orthogonal geometries that work to support the idea of connectedness. The overall effect is one of a general *ropiness*, as though the building was composed of the slightly disinterested or careless repositioning of something akin to an enormous rectangular garden hose, ineffectively concealed by the wrapper.

Cohen often conflates continuity of the surface with the continuity of line. It is a strategy that can be found in roped pottery (13) and is a continuing trait in his work. It is almost as if one of Sheeler's factory compositions of discrete volumes and kinetic diagonals has been reproduced as an interior, but shrink-wrapped by the continuous surface of the exterior in an attempt to 'hide' the complexity of the volumes within the reduced complexity of the skin.

Shapes and their attendant arguments begin to emerge. Although Taiyuan's 'rope' argues for a general continuity because it is a line and because the building is discrete, by implication there must be ends—two at a minimum. And although the exact nature of the

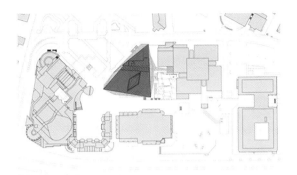

8 Amir Building, Tel Aviv Museum of Art, Preston Scott Cohen, 2003-11

9

10 Fahmy House, Preston Scott Cohen, 2007, 2016

11 Goodman House, Preston Scott Cohen, 2001-04

12

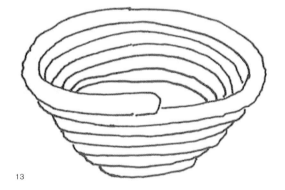

13

ropes disposition is not immediately clear, one of the candidates for an end is immediately apparent. This candidate is aggressively offered in the form of the gigantic cantilever extended out toward the park above the museum's main entry plaza (14). This is one of the ways that Cohen produces distinct particularities within a general vocabulary of continuity, at least with regard to his larger projects. A similar condition occurs in Tel Aviv, where a rope ends on the north facade (15). A simpler manifestation can be found at Nanjing, where the ends of the rope reveal themselves almost immediately, in a De Stijl-like XYZ reverie (16).

Given an initial impression that the facades at Taiyuan are not tightly organized, the existence and positioning of the cantilever is somewhat surprising in that one of the resultant readings of the facade is that the basic organization has more than just a passing similarity to its classical predecessors. The cantilever (which one will eventually discover to be the restaurant) acts in many ways like the central portico in a traditional Beaux Arts plan: it is more or less in the middle and serves to mark the main entry from the park. It also argues that the rest of the building defers, to some degree, to the park's symmetry while offering wings to the left and right of itself (17).

The effect is enhanced when one moves to the west and the slight difference between the two sides is corrected by the effects of perspective. One of the most striking views is from the front of the building on the complex's central axis. From this perspective, the low facade to the left of the cantilever seems to defer to the portico as it drops a limp wrist to touch the central axis (18). This view also reveals a candidate for the other end of the rope in the form of the limp wrist, an argument that is reinforced by the fact that it reveals itself at the exact spot that marks the center of the portico. It seems that the beginning and ending of the ropiness, after all of the layering and looping, have moved back to complete a figure and achieve closure. One is reminded of similar devices in other buildings, such as the plan version of the argument found at La Tourette (19).

One of the qualities of the skin at Taiyuan is the changing pattern of panelization. In most places, the skin consists of horizontally rectangular panels with stacked joints (which further 'betrays' the interior layering). Sometimes this system is superimposed

upon another system of super-triangulation that performs two contradictory tasks: it unifies the skin as though it were contained within a larger system of netting by binding the rectangular elements more tightly together, while—because it is not a continuous system—implying discrete components within the skin. In the latter case, it reinforces the reading of the tube structure. There is a third condition where, absent the diagonal superstructure, the rectangular panels seem to delaminate and form horizontal laminations (20). This continues a theme of the facade acting like a surface that decomposes into the linearity of the ropes while the linearity of the ropes delaminates into the linearity of the strings. This is the condition that happens to mark both ends of the tube system as revealed on the facade. The surfaces of both the cantilever and the limp wrist can be seen delaminating into linear layers. The viewer is encouraged to look at these pieces as though they were literally the fraying ends of a rope, the whole of it reinforcing a basic reading of the building's organization via the rope trope.

From this perspective in particular, the building best reveals the evolution of one of its basic arguments. Although it initially seems an amorphous pile, it is actually composed of layered tubes that coil about only to reveal that they are, in fact, a single line, ultimately expressed in the discovery of the two ends. As a single line, it suggests the basic organization of the building as well as one strategy of how circulation through it will be achieved. The entry view indicates that as far as the front facade is concerned, the building seems to consist of linear elements. It is possible that they are all components of a single long tube that snakes around, starting at the ground just to the left of the entry and with a bit of unseen wrapping, loops to the upper right and finishes back in the center (on the roof) as the projecting restaurant. The whole of it makes a loose sort of figure eight, sheared to produce a top and a bottom as well as a beginning and an end.

In fact, only parts of this proposition are completely true. There *is* a spiraling route that will move one up through the building. It is also true that one ultimately arrives at the cantilevering restaurant and that the disposition of the program of the building does in fact form a figure eight. But some of the other readings are a bit deceptive, or perhaps better put, nuanced references. First of all, one doesn't enter the building by

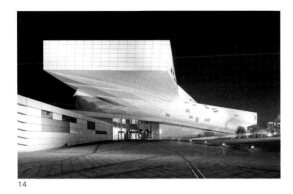

14

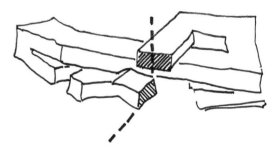

18

15

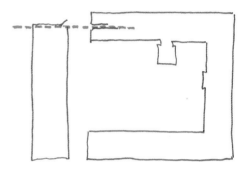

19

16 Nanjing University Student Center, 2006-08

20

17

accessing the limp wrist. Furthermore, it turns out not to be the other end of the tubular system anyway. The actual plan of the building reveals that the tubes themselves are a bit of a deception, especially toward the bottom of the building and especially to the west, where the two major galleries are *not* really linked together. In fact, no clear or singular candidate for the second terminus of the rope ever presents itself.

The rope does make an appearance, however. The basic elements of the plan configuration at Taiyuan reveal that, for the most part, they are linearly organized and agglomerated bits, where the bits seem to be fragments of an orthogonal fabric and the agglomeration has a lot to do with the insistent connectivity of the outer perimeter. As such, there are strong similarities with other organizations, including not just buildings, but also landscapes and urban typologies. In the case of buildings, one type that strikes a resonant note is that of the castle, particularly when it comes to the plan. The insistence that the single perimeter wall encircle, enclose, and defend a particular space is at odds with the interests of the multitude of particular enclosed programmatic elements that want to be coherent in themselves (21). Other schemes, such as Moore's Kresge College, might have ropey properties, but the individuality of the organized pieces still reads strongly (22).

At Tiayuan, the rope is internally organized by the pathway (23). Mont San Michele is a bit of both: the pathway ropes are differentiated by the topography of the hill as well as by the transition from edge to center (24). At least in terms of its plan, McKim, Mead, and White's Narragansett Pier (25) could almost be a fragment of the Taiyuan project. Part of the appeal of each of these schemes is the contrast between the coherence of the overall form and the articulation and seeming indifference of the particular pieces that make up the form. The Taiyuan Museum achieves a similar appeal through both the contrast of the exterior skin with the interior fragmentation as well as the contrast between the fragmentation of the pieces and the unity of the circulation.

Large museums require a lot of internal navigation and the elevation of the Tiayuan Museum acts as a clue for the basic template of the building's essential circulation. The viewer would be correct in surmising that the route through the building will be, at its heart, a continuous pathway that will end at the top with the restaurant. One begins by entering the building under the restaurant

cantilever and through the doors directly ahead into the huge atrium, around which the right tubing wraps. This is the right half of the figure eight. To the left, however, one notices an equivalent space: the outdoor courtyard embraced by the westernmost roping. This conforms to the symmetries implied by the façade and indicates that the building is split between two equal-ish halves that are similar but different, a plan that is similar to a large domino. This western end of the building is conceptually tied, at least by basic orientation, to the other buildings that form the Wall of Culture and that encircle the park, the 'Gang of Four.' The eastern end is free from this obligation and has a slightly more independent geometry. Here, we see the remnants of the cityside/parkside strategy not so evident in the larger context (26). The use of this strategy as a termination is not uncommon (e.g., Gehry's Air and Space Museum) and is best represented here, in plan, at ground level. The perimeter walls on the right attempt to wrap some sort of center that is relatively indifferent to orthogonal geometry whereas the walls on the left seem to respond more to the orthogonal delineation of the boundaries. This is evidenced by the parallel walls and by the centralizing geometry of the east-west axis, to which the dimple on the western facade seems to be in service (27). As with Tel Aviv, this strategy reveals the dexterity with which Cohen can use the seeming sameness of the universal surface of the facade to achieve radically different effects and create gestures of either urban connectivities or indifferent disconnectivities. At this level, the building's halves are paired as both equal and opposite. They are two wrapped courtyards embraced by the building's wrapper. One courtyard is an interior atrium while the other is an exterior space: a vague reminiscence of Bramante's Palazzo Cancelleria (28).

Within the same system of perimeter cladding, the western half embraces aspects of an overall orthogonality and axiality while the eastern half supports a more loosely centric and independent organizational scheme. Internally, these differences persist. Within the western half, the interior facades of the courtyard splay in sympathy to one another and to a central axis that unites the building with the adjacent representative of the Gang of Four to produce the relatively familiar shape of an equilateral triangle. The interior of the eastern half seems to be a relatively disorganized void formed by a variety of unrelated, isolated, and disarrayed pieces

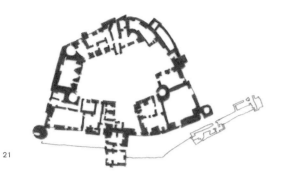

21

25

22

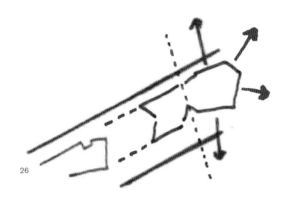

26

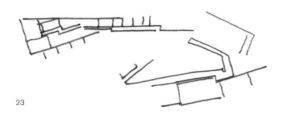

23

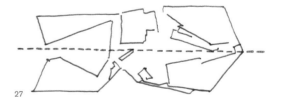

27

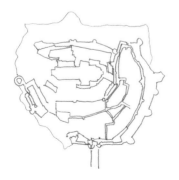

24

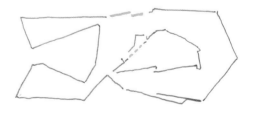

28

around it (29). These contrasting strategies are at least partially reconciled by the fact that the east and west exterior elevations seem to be inverses of each other and that the protrusion at the east end could easily be accommodated by the dimple on the west, as if the building were in essence a large section of Brio, the toy wooden railroad track. In this respect, each of the two halves of the building appear to replicate the other in a similar fashion, with the easternmost elements of the western piece imitating the eastern piece and vice versa, as though a section of track has in fact already been assembled (30).

The axis of the figure eight connects the two courtyards and creates a zipper-like organization within the building, breaking all the lateral connections of the figure eight and allowing the various spaces along the spine of the plan to be both differentiated and connected (31). The effect is similar to a sequence of urban plazas that are connected by a series of sightlines and gateways, suggesting that the strategy that worked so successfully on the exterior of Tel Aviv has been used to help organize the interior at Taiyuan. According to this reading, relatively small spaces can assume larger significance. The circulation area immediately to the left of the entry from the park, which occupies the center of the figure eight and is relatively small, is the element that visually connects the two main spaces of the domino: the courtyard and the atrium (32). This circulation area is also the vestibule that connects these spaces to the circulation and to the primary elevator core, which, although seemingly minor, makes it the heart of the building in terms of both horizontal and vertical movement. Although a major connector, it is oriented in such a way as to diminish the visual connection from east to west and acts as a sort of cork in the bottle of the space of the west courtyard. To some degree it provides the same service to the southern entry, to which it announces its relationship but hides its significance (33). The openings in the perimeter to the north, east, and south help to situate the building in its context and add to the pavilionization of this half of the Domino. These openings also reinforce the independence of the building fragments that hold the program in the form of the auditorium and the majority of the galleries.

Although they might be seen as de rigueur elements in the design of the contemporary art museum, giant atria have been a common feature of art museums for hundreds of years and their purpose has been to impress, to be sure. But they were also needed to organize the plan conceptually and to allow for any vertical circulation that was immediately adjacent while bringing natural light deep within the interior of the building. All of these roles remain present at Taiyuan, but the twist here is that this is neither the only open space nor the sole organizational model for the entire plan. The Zipper addresses this situation by positioning the atrium as one of a sequence of related spaces. It also helps to reconcile the vertical emphasis of both the courtyard and the atrium with the need for each to accommodate themselves within a unifying system of horizontal movement. It ultimately proves to be the means of initiating the ramping system of circulation.

At the easternmost end of the museum is the lobby auditorium: a space that is both part of the larger sequence and separate from it. It maintains direct access to the outside, allowing the auditorium to operate independently from the rest of the building. To reinforce this independence and to deal with the topography of the site, the elevation of this lobby is significantly below that of the atrium. Its relative separation is also underscored by a crinkle in the perimeter wall that tends to idealize this lobby as a piece separate from the swath of the zipper (34). To access this area from the interior, both a stair and a ramp extend down to it from the atrium. This is, in effect, the beginning of the ramp system that is the basic circulation organizer for the building (and a further candidate for the beginning of the rope). The stairs move quickly into the space of the atrium while the ramp naturally extends farther and terminates near the gap that separates the auditorium fragment. Here it meets another ramp that leads from the atrium floor to the upper levels of program, allowing the lower segment to integrate seamlessly with its upper brethren (35). Immediately across the atrium to the west is a colonnade that eats into the volume at the base of the western fragment of the domino. This signals the continuation of circulation from the ramp system into the central knuckle and then on to the galleries to the west (36). In essence, this knuckle subtly locks together the two courtyards. As much as an effort is being made to link the pieces of the building together, there is an alternative strategy to fragment the building into pieces.

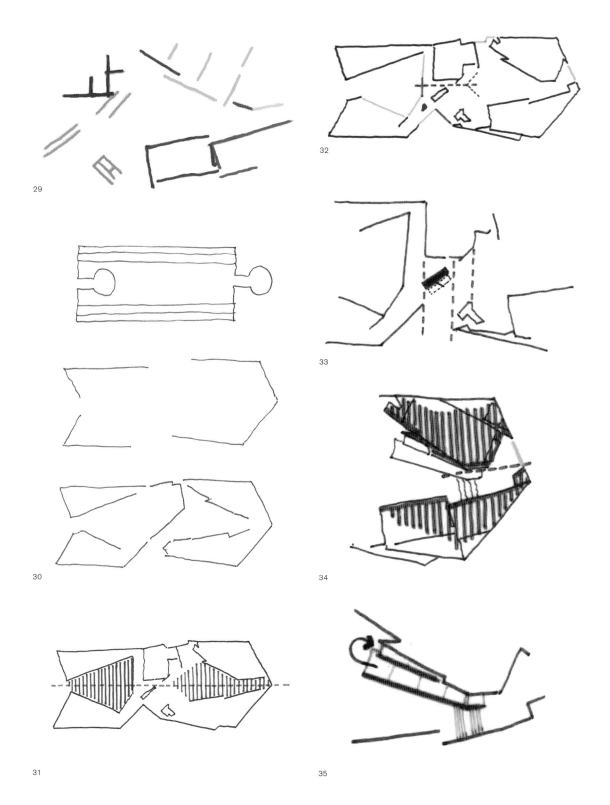

29

30

31

32

33

34

35

This is not just the disparate fragments of program that are seemingly scattered along the axis, but also the suggested voids defined between them, which constitute another series of spaces (37). This tends to formulate smaller pieces of orderliness in what might be seen as a chaotic system. In addition, it creates areas that link the building to the various exterior vistas, leaving one more contained space at the very center of the building, between the north and south entries.

The seemingly casual organization of the eastern pavilions allows a multitude of alternative readings to be formulated. The strategy would be very familiar to Camillo Sitte and is reflected in many of his diagrams that research the ways in which irregular spaces make complex arguments for spatial readings. Rather than merely existing as oddly disorganized and vaguely picturesque, these types of space have the ability to articulate intricate narratives of which their more geometrically precise siblings are incapable. In this regard, Cohen is part of that large army of current designers who are able to introduce a sort of Crypto-Medievalism into their projects. Diamond Ranch High School by Morphosis (38) might be one example and Eisenman's City of Culture in Santiago de Compostela another, in which case it is literally Crypto-Medieval, as the outline of the streets of the old city have been buried in the landscape of the new site. At any rate, this is a strategy which is a current—if relatively unacknowledged—mainstay in design studios.

At Taiyuan, the device works in multiple ways that allow the visitor to be informed about various relationships and nuances that elaborate upon arguments in the building. For example, within the general cacophony of the atrium, an area at each corner emerges to be a coherent space in its own right (39). These spaces (the entry to the south, the lower stairway landing to the east, the ramp access to the north) act as circulation and access hubs. The entire program along the southern facade of the museum could be read as a continuous bar, merely fractured at the entry and in support of the Zipper idea (40). We could read the two halves of the domino as having slipped or rotated along a shear line to form two independent components of the atrium (41). We could read the north facade of the courtyard as a continuation of the outer perimeter wall, but folded inside (42). We could read the same wall as the continuation of the north interior wall of the atrium, with all the back-of-house programs demurely hidden within all of the other readings and functioning as the figural central node within what is, in reality, one giant open space (43). The bends and twists also serve to allow the movement through the space to constantly change the basic idea of how the space is configured. This choreographed experience of the building is not a single narrative but a series of counterpoints. The current impression regarding the organization of the museum is quickly superseded by another, and yet another, as layer is added to layer to create a complex and nuanced system of readings.

The zipper not only links a sequence of spaces while establishing a consistency and normalcy within the hyperactivity of the plan, but it also creates a datum that allows one to measure progress through the building via a system of reference points that lend significance to moments along the path, such as when the elevator pairs cross the narrow chasm at the eastern extension of the atrium (44). This area serves as another version of the knuckle of the vestibule and acts as a competitive node of vertical access that links the second, third, and fourth floor galleries while absorbing the stairway that leads down to the auditorium. On the third and fourth floors, the dominant knuckle moves to a location above the main entry to where the surprise of a secret garden defines and contains the central atrium and allows the space to extend to the facade. This area is where the public lounge is located and acts as a local base for those visitors on the upper levels. The lounge allows for the first view through the perimeter wall since leaving the ground level, a view back across the park to the Gang of Four, and the hint of another view into the western courtyard.

Just to the west of this area is a lobby with views into the exterior courtyard. There are formal similarities between this area and both the visitor lounge and the secret garden, each one creating mirrored lobes surrounding the adjacent circulation core. This is one of a number of instances in which the various components of the building create local mirrorings within a system that seems to support larger ambiguities, many of which are on this floor alone (45). The purpose of this strategy seems to be to create a new reading of the front facade where a portion that faces the park bends inward to become the eastern facade of the courtyard (46). This strategy further turns the vertical circulation core into a

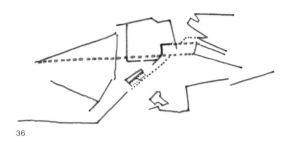

36

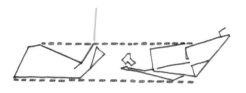

40

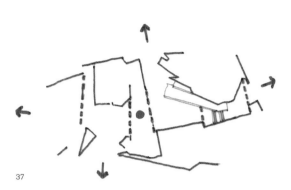

37

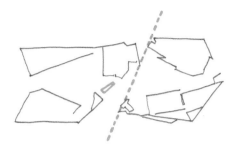

41

38

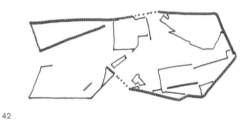

42

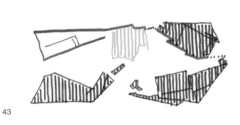

43

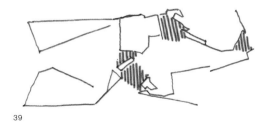

39

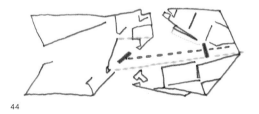

44

central component of the building that serves as both a connector and a separator of the voids of the figure eight (47). The use of mirroring here lends emphasis to the secret garden as more than just a pleasant interlude. The garden is a major organizer of the scheme and suggests a new axis that is centered on the curved perimeter and almost manages to penetrate to the outside (48).

The effect is to suggest that the atrium, rather than being completely wrapped by the roping, is composed of an assembly of separate pavilions that are barely connected at the corners. The arrangement is vaguely reminiscent of organizations of buildings around a public square, such as a loose version of the Karolinenplatz along Briennerstrasse. It suggests a linear armature of experiences, the sequence of spaces of varying geometries, and the dichotomy that exists between an organization of a universal street wall and individual buildings as objects. All of these similarities create echoes that seem to connect the two projects, as if the Munich ensemble had been folded back on itself by means of a number of twists and bends (49). At any rate, the suggestion that the sort of urban fabric found in the exterior arrangement of Briennerstrasse is found to a large extent as interior phenomena in the Taiyuan Museum is perhaps not too far off the mark. It perhaps reflects the predilections of our age for complex spaces as well as the difficulty of positing coherent urban design strategies in the contemporary city beyond the boundaries of a single project. Clearly, recent Chinese urban expansions such as Taiyuan have exemplified this problem, but it can be found embedded in a wide range of first world developments: La Defense, Ground Zero, anything even vaguely near Canary Wharf, etc.

It's also interesting that as Cohen exploits the potential formal uses of this device he is either re-inventing or returning to design strategies that seem somewhat outside current interests. One of these might be the use in English Landscape of moments which suggest closure and continuation, such as the use of tree lines to both bound a space and imply its extension into adjoining spaces, a device Olmstead used numerous times. This could almost be a definition of Tiayuan's courtyard formulation. Another example somewhat far afield might be found in the formal organization of English villages, a sort of down-market

version of Sitte. The sort of triangular village green such as found at Snowshill might be surreptitiously substituted into the Tiayuan plan with no immediate injury of the museum's scheme (50).

A third compatriot would be various features of natural landscapes, especially since geomorphology is a bit more mainline at the moment as a legitimate source of inspiration and study. In the void version, cleft valleys, such as Antelope Canyon off the Colorado, share a similar quality with Taiyuan in the dilemma they pose: are they formed from two different objects brought in close proximity to create the valley, or is the valley itself figural and the material to either side merely subject to its carving (51). The solid version might be found in the geological equivalent of the twisting street-walls of Snowshill, the syncline fold. Particularly good versions can be found in Pennsylvania, in the area between Altoona and Williamsport, an area which could reasonably be called the Cohen Range. Brush Hill, near the southern edge of the system, is a spectacular example of the bending bar that seems to be derived from the same formal interests as the Taiyuan project.

In a similar vein, another strategy that is particularly noticeable in the scheme is the variety of ways in which the concept of boundary is used. Two of these uses involve the collision of two systems to form one entity. The first involves those areas in which the interior walls are aligned with one perimeter but bracketed by another. The southeast galleries, for example, express the distinction between the orthogonal system on the interior and its collision with the unifying perimeter wrapper of a very different geometry (52). This will have a significant impact on the experience and understanding of the nature of the organization. The local orthogonal organizations found in the building virtually never align with the exterior wall. The lone exception occurs on the northern edge of the courtyard, although perhaps this signals that this is where the exterior turns inward (53). It is a situation that occurs all over the building: interior-exterior organizations are opposed and many of the spaces that result are the consequences of these juxtapositions and collisions. These fragments of interiority are largely responsible for creating the edges of the atrium and courtyard that—although they seem to imitate the exterior condition—are produced by an alternative system. One result of this condition is

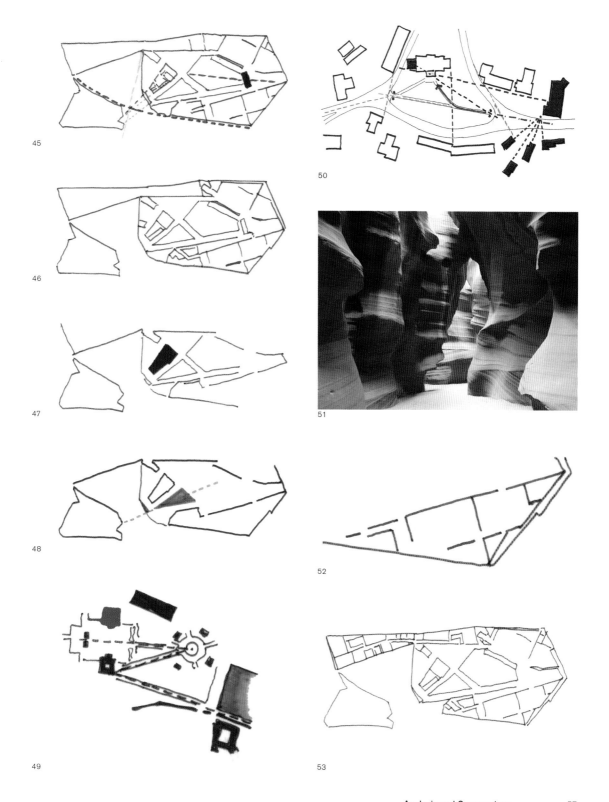

45

46

47

48

49

50

51

52

53

the encouragement of reading of the building as the result of some sort of transformation, the fragmented evidence of which is written in the pieces (54).

Another manifestation of the collision of boundaries involves the interpenetration of one space into another by way of overlapping. This seems to happen more on the upper floors, as if the building were increasing in porosity and spatial complexity as one nears the top of the spiraling progression. There is an example near the visitor's lounge, where walls that appear to be significant spatial dividers can also be read as internal to other spatial systems (55).

The basic organization of the plan and the condition of the perimeter facade suggest that the building could offer multiple arguments for its development through some form of transformative genesis, each involving a simple origin. As one relatively simple possibility, the design may have started with a relatively ideal bar-like organization that, through a series of twists and folds, has been reconfigured to form something akin to a Figure 8 (56). On a macro level, this 'history' would explain how the plan has come to be both a domino and a pretzel and how the relative height differences of the two western arms came about. On a micro level, this would also explain why the plan consists of clumps of rectangular fragments contained within a continuous skin; the skin records the bending and folding and the fragments refer to an original, uniform rectangular bar structure.

At the opposite end of the spectrum, there might be some cause to read the scheme as the elaborate transformation of another ideal figure, the palazzo (57a-f). Like an alternative version of a chess game, through a series of transformations and disruptions, the components of the palazzo—the perimeter, the corners, the cortile, the center—are gradually separated and reconfigured (in response to program, site, Feng Shui, whatever…) to create a more expressive, differentiated, and particular composition. The emerging figure explores the potential of new relationships and allegiances in an arrangement of more independent components, while still maintaining some aspects of the original geometry. As a result, the scheme permits remnants of ideality which impart a certain authority and essential organization to the building, while at the same time allowing the expression of individual components and highly differentiated moments based on their unique ordering schemes especially when freed from each other.

As a result of this reorganization, there emerges a new sort of center on the eastern perimeter, where the major walls both interior and exterior are radial to one point, while at the western end becomes an opening, a new center on the western perimeter, in deference to the building's lateral axis. In essence, this describes the evolution of the building's domino scheme. Although the plan has become increasingly eccentric, there are still manifestations of the original, ideal scheme, not just in the survival of the individual components, but in the maintenance of their basic geometries and some surviving adherence to their original relationships. Thus, the galleries, although dispersed compositionally, are still similarly composed and, although increasingly independent in their configuration, still support the 'original,' ideal relationship as evidenced in the survival of a sort of quincuncial configuration. Furthermore, the shard-like pieces of the western gallery arms would fit exactly into the courtyard formed by the corresponding two eastern arms, to reinforce the idea that they were evidencing some sort of displacement from a simpler original figure (58). The hexagonal organization that is embraced by the building has the triple advantage of suggesting not only the elongation of an original ideal square into a more complex and differentiated composition, but this geometry also encourages the emergence of the continuous perimeter, while at the same time creating a connection with the motif of the larger site plan of the park in which the museum is situated, which also incorporates an unfolding hexagon with square aspirations.

As the visitor spirals higher into the museum, the nature of the architecture shifts in a number of ways. The sense of enclosure changes as areas that (on lower levels) would have been voids between perimeter fragments now close up while new openings appear. One example is at the northern corner of the atrium on the second floor, where the office wing is allowed to attach itself to the northeast galleries via the freight elevator (59). It isn't clear why this is a useful device here programmatically, but formally it strengthens the unity of the northern facade and begins to congeal the upper levels of the atrium into a more solid ring.

As one continues the rise, new vistas appear across the atrium to reveal shifts and turns. One might expect

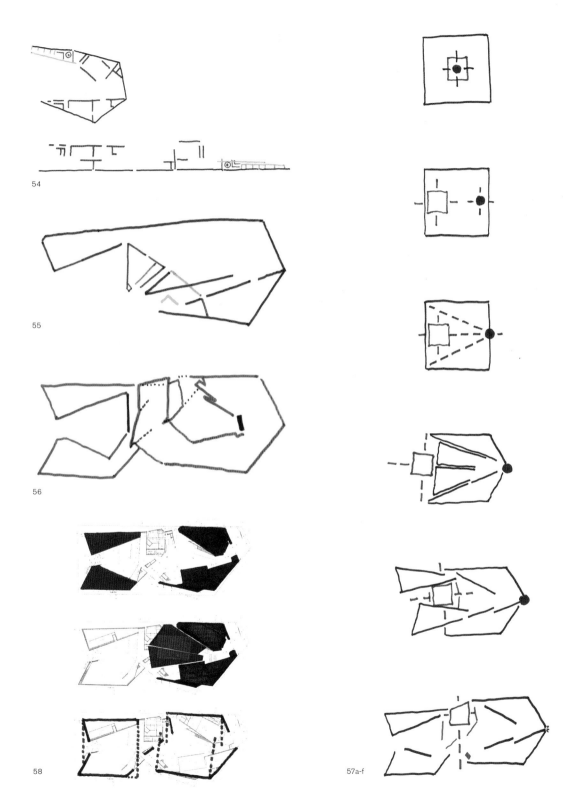

54

55

56

58

57a-f

some of these changes to occur as the circulation route nears the roof. After all, the roof isn't just another ceiling for the particular fragments, but is instead a part of the all-encompassing perimeter which will attempt to lock everything back together as part of the single surface facade. Another reason for such architectural shifts and changes is that, unless the restaurant is the particular goal of the visitor, the constant specificity of a single line of circulation makes less and less sense. There is a need to find some way to disperse the visitor into the various galleries and allow for a graceful way to reverse course and return to the lobby. Dispersal is encouraged three times over: by the protrusion of the secret garden, by the connection of the atrium to the exterior through the garden and the waiting area, and by the displacement of the pathway system to each side of the garden. Each of these dispersal-prompts require the visitor to acknowledge the exterior in a ritual of closure before continuing to the final galleries, which as a result can be seen as a sort of surprise bonus, like the small reserve gas tank on an old Volkswagen. Although these galleries essentially adjoin the northern facade, no particular gesture to capitalize on that connection takes place. Recognizing that one had returned to this facade might have been used to reorient the visitor and to acknowledge that the sequence was nearing its end and the game was over.

A different strategy does much the same thing, however. After perusing the final galleries, the visitor arrives in the ultimate space that could be a gallery, but it is formed completely differently. It is not the fragment of an orthogonal system but is, instead, completely triangular and offers no clues as to its allegiance or orientation. It has an independence as if it were a third micro-courtyard formed by the collision of things around it similar to the main courtyards. A further sense of dispersal occurs here as a result of the ambiguity of a configuration that tends to open the triangular space out to the adjacent courtyard. Does the exterior wall belong to it? To the façade? Is it an isolated element that divides this area from the courtyard (60)? Inside this room is the "object stairway," a sculptural piece that is completely unlike any other stairway in the building and essentially becomes part of the permanent collection. As such, it weds the building's architecture permanently to its collection of art, somewhat akin to the Venturi column in his Oberlin addition (61).

In addition the stair helps to effectuate the effortless change of course, creating an invitation to begin the descent, first to the galleries below and then down the ramp back to the lobby. Not only is this element caught between the worlds of architecture and art, it is also trapped between the ancient and the modern, as it seems reminiscent of both the a medieval stairway that might be found in a Norman castle as well as something more immediately contemporary—something that might be attributed to Sol Lewitt. It is as if the stairway not only helps redirect us towards the lobby, but also returns us to the building's source in a primitive version of a spiral stairway.

Although it is clear that the main circulation primarily spirals throughout the building as a single coil, at moments, particularly the bottom and top, the single route branches into a number of alternatives. This performs a number of tasks. It serves to break the monotony of the system while maintaining its basic clarity and it allows gallery spaces that are not part of the circulation helix to be incorporated easily into the system. It also allows the spiral to be a suggestion but not an inevitability, so for example, all visitors aren't ultimately directed into the restaurant. The situation on the lower level is similar in that the pathway that descends the ramp into the atrium can be seen continuing down to the adjacent ramp to the auditorium lobby, or it can move out into the atrium, where the other corners also suggest extension of the system. Thus a diagram for the totality might start to look like that of a tree, with a root system below matched by a branch system above, but held together by a single trunk. Unlike the tree, the 'roots and branches' of Tiayuan aren't strictly linear and branching, but form more complex configurations, but the building's trunk-like quality holds everything together. On the ground level, one moves off the courtyard, or on the upper levels, off the atrium, to explore the galleries, which are slightly more complex and differentiated. After brief sojourns in the micro-labyrinths, and after a few surprises, one returns to the certainty of the helix (62). It's like a three dimensional version of a banjo, with an unchanging drone string allowing one to more easily chart the melodic structures. The three diagrams of helix, double courtyards, and a variety of extended circulation pieces congeal to allow the building to function as what could best be described as 'a maze on domino.'

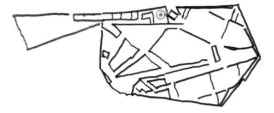

59

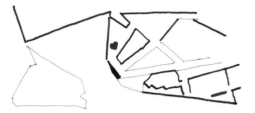

60

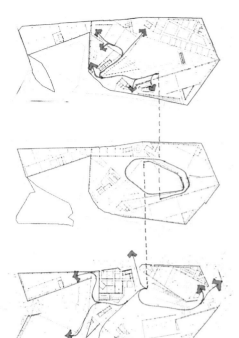

62

61

The way in which the circulation routes fray and weave back together is reminiscent of yet another aspect of both nature and the vernacular: the former in regard to riparian systems of meandering channels and islands; the latter in the form of interweaving pathway systems of the village, as in this example from Broadway (63).

Also similar to both, but perhaps a bit more automotive in nature, it can be argued that Hadid's MAXXI Museum might be a sibling of Taiyuan, at least as far as a shared interest in particular elements of the diagram, but in Rome the clear use of the tubular structures for both circulation and galleries prevents alternative strategies for exhibition spaces to be employed and the tubes have no particularly clear relationships to each other (64). If they are meant to constitute a single system, the system has been fractured and fragmented into what essentially results in a labyrinthine pile.

Above the main floor, the manner in which circulation and galleries are organized seems to have an aversion to wrapping as one might expect. Because of the position of the offices, the route that connects the second floor galleries along the north side can only be achieved by the insertion of a special bridge that jumps across the corner of the atrium, as though the atrium had to be stapled together. On the third floor, the galleries open into what seems to be a lobby for the offices. Each of these situations transforms the notion of the unbroken wrapper (observed on the elevation) into a giant *P* in plan (65). One can escape it the first time by means of the bridge, but the second encounter proves unavoidable. This area, along with the restaurant is also a candidate for where one comes to the end of one's rope.

Given the rest of the plan, the shape of the perimeter, and the small scale of the western galleries, the P plan redirects the attention that was previously paid to the facade of the museum to the southwest, as though it were genuflecting back to the central building of the complex. This tends to further cut off the southwestern gallery from the rest of the composition and heighten its exceptional status.

This area continues a theme found throughout the building: one moves through the museum via areas that seemed peripheral and of little importance only to have them emerge in a new light as important moments and significant organizers. The alignment of the curving edge of the southern courtyard seems interested in maintaining the general curve of the southeastern perimeter facade, as though the southwestern gallery is being cut off from the rest of the composition (66). In a counter gesture, the configuration of the upper gallery walls in this area indicate some connection with the main part of the atrium areas, particularly the orientations and geometries of the circulation corridors around the lounge. In general, the third level plan seems to support the idea that the lower and western portions of the building—and the southwestern gallery in particular—have been cast adrift as the pathway folds upwards and back to the center, much like Mont San Michele (67).

The first art museums were palaces and therefore organized primarily around a single main floor, although usually raised one floor off the ground. This strategy was more or less the model for subsequent variants, especially when factoring in the need for proper day lighting as in the Pinakothek. It also served as a valuable model for museums in which the main floor was at ground level, like Dulwich. Schinkel's Altes Museum in Berlin (68) altered this formula by providing for two floors of exhibition space that were connected by a spacious stair-hall that provided views back over the city. The difference underscores the ability to pack a lot more program into a limited space by moving vertically, but also the long-standing affection for a single main floor, even in tall buildings.

A focused interest in the interior stairway's architectural possibilities occurred surprisingly late in Western architecture. A comparison between the exterior and interior stair systems at Villa Rotunda underscores the distinction. The former are grand, historically referential, and celebrate the experience, while the latter are a bit mean, cramped, and residual (69). Medieval architecture does provide some fine examples, but these tend to connect only two floors and to accommodate what is essentially a single modulating floor plan.

Baroque architecture is generally considered to have addressed these oversights with a vengeance, particularly in the form of the German stair-halls. Neumann's example at the Würzburg Residenz (70), although initially exceptional, was destined to become the ubiquitous solution. In the previous

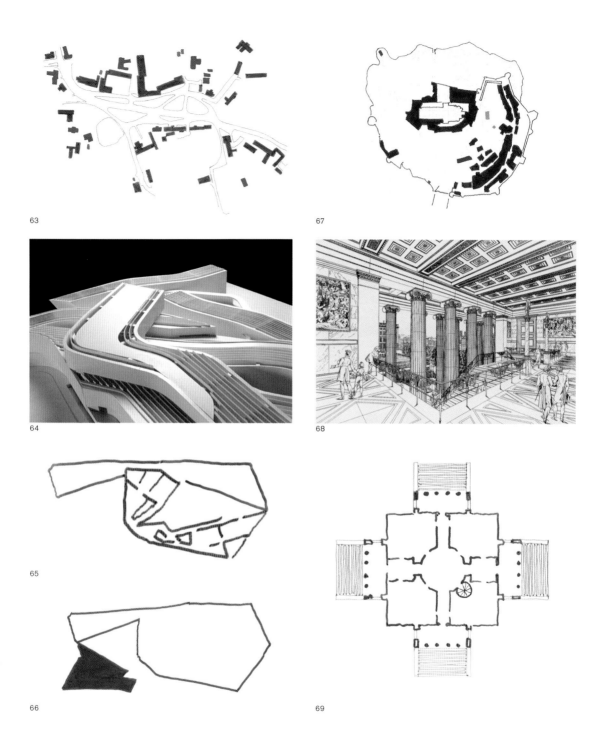

63

64

65

66

67

68

69

century, Mannerist architects enthusiastically adapted Bramante's helical ramp system for the Vatican to produce a series of amazing spiral stairways, including those at Amboise and Chambord. The former was particularly useful programmatically, as it gave soldiers on horseback easy access between the riverfront and the hilltop upon which the chateau sat. The latter was amazing in the physical and experiential sense and provided dramatic circulation with spectacular views into and out of the structure (71). It existed simultaneously as an object in space as well as a void and it could be seen as a possible inspiration for the columns in Ito's Mediatheque in Sendai (72). These projects exemplify the differentiation of vertical pathway schemes into two categories: those motivated by programmatic need (Type A), and those more interested in providing an interesting experience (Type B).

Projects that fall into the Type A category could provide for a variety of needs; similar structures for similar purposes were constructed at Orvietto (for a siege well, in 1527) and Dover (for troop movements, in 1807). Orvietto was a double helix, while Dover was triple. In each case, they broke the model that would be formulated by the stair-hall and instead argued for a continuous system that did not distinguish between particular floors while manifesting a strategy that could be extended indefinitely over huge heights. Both Orvietto and Dover covered a vertical difference of approximately 180 feet. In addition to corkscrewing spirals, non-helical ramps were incorporated into architecture, often as components in fortifications such as Perugia's Rocca Paolina, which incorporated pre-existing streets within its bulk.

These systems paved the way for numerous industrial and commercial applications in the 19th and 20th centuries, from the taxi ramps at St. Pancras Station in London to the animal gangways at the slaughterhouse in Shanghai, which, although certainly picturesque, appear to have been motivated by programmatic concerns (73). The alternative trajectory was motivated almost purely for the delight of the experience.

Projects that fall into the Type B category might include the 18th century follies associated with English Landscape: the tunnel systems at Stourhead, West Wycombe Park, Scott's Grotto (74), and the incredible tunnel system that comprises the Grand Cascade

in the Bois de Boulogne in Paris, whereby two lakes at different elevations are connected by tunnels for both water and pedestrians in an elaborate system of choreography by which virtually every possible combination is explored and put into a narrative (of *together*, *separate*, *under*, *over*, and *in*) before the pathway emerges under a waterfall in an underground cave with a view into the lower lake.

Projects of this kind were part of the inspiration for Olmstead's decision to separate the pathway systems in Central Park by varying the section and were later incorporated into the Modernist mantra regarding the separation of various pathway systems that aimed to be always useful and sometimes surprising and delightful. An integration of the two types can be found in the use of helical stairways in modern architecture. Tecton's Penguin Pools (75) at the London Zoo are a canonic example and ended up being a device that Niemeyer could hardly resist (76) although the penguins proved not to be big fans. Types A and B continued to be conflated in examples like the Vatican Museum of 1932, 427 years after Bramante's original. In a way, although iconically modern, Wright's use of the device at the Guggenheim is closer in spirit to Bramante as a wide ramp rather than a stair, since it allows the surrounding walls to be used for display purposes. Bramante's design included niches that were presumably intended for a similar purpose.

Certainly the Taiyuan Art Museum project will conjure images of the Guggenheim if one were to attempt to chart a genealogy of influence for the building. As wonderful as the Guggenheim is, the experience is a bit repetitive and spatially limiting. Taiyuan is constantly changing and, although the people-watching opportunities may be equal to those at the Guggenheim in New York, the experience of the circulation is far more complex and varied. Unlike the Guggenheim, at Taiyuan one can imagine that there might be particularly favorite moments or that a visitor might want to reveal the pathway's secrets to friends. It's hard to imagine that there is a particular place along the ramp in the Guggenheim that selfies are taken, while at Taiyuan one expects they will sort themselves into a concentration of specific moments.

It has already been remarked upon that, with regard to many features—a folded perimeter, fragmented orthogonal pieces of program, productively

70

71

72

73

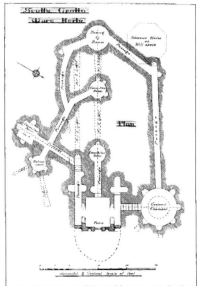

74

A plan of the grotto made in 1900 by Mr R.T. Andrews, of the East Herts Archaeological Society – with amendments to show the new porch.

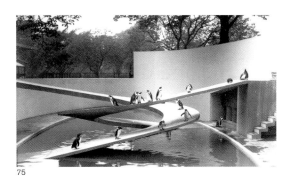

75

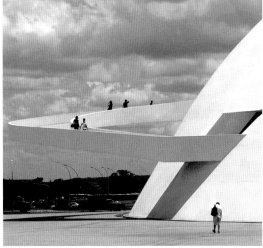

76

irregular courtyards, a continuous pathway system, a fabulous complexity, and a seemingly unstudied picturesqueness—the Taiyuan Musuem is surprisingly similar to the late Romantic castle. It is easy to imagine that Taiyuan was meant to be exceptional, visitable, and picturesque, and the Romantic castles had many of the same characteristics. Many of these features could be found in the original sources, but in the Romantic versions they were supremely organized to produce theatrically stupendous effects. Although many Romantic castles were completely original, some, like Chantilly or Arundel, were built inside or on the ruins of the real thing. These are forced to deal with the difficult fragmented geometries of the original as best they can, while the new-builds employed similar geometries to increase the picturesqueness and to create wonderfully nuanced and changing relationships between the various elements, like Tiayuan. They are particularly effective in orchestrating the sequence of movement into and through the major exterior parts of the castle, morphing to something only a bit more architecturally familiar on the interior.

What is particularly interesting is the way the entry sequences in these cases is organized to great effect, as theatrical entertainment on the one hand, and as a way to fragment smaller scale spaces and objects from the larger ensemble. A selection of examples share this particular strategy of orchestrating the arrival sequence via ramps and bridges and using it to create subspaces and to separate pavilions from what had appeared to be a massive and tight agglomeration.

But perhaps the example that is closest to the spirit of Taiyuan, especially in terms of circulation, is found at the Hohenzollern Castle at Hechingen (77). Built in the mid-19th century, the castle is almost pointless except for its political statement after the formation of a unified Germany as a Prussian landmark in non-Prussian south Germany. It could be used as a summer home except that it is in the middle of nowhere and has access to nothing in particular. It is meant to be seen and visited but not really to be lived in. As a result, it is designed primarily for the interest of the experience, not unlike many contemporary museums, and nowhere more so than the delight of the entry sequence. After climbing to the top of an isolated mountainous lump, the visitor arrives at what will prove to be merely the first gateway.

There will be four more gates and three more entry plazas, each separated by a spiraling ramp system that is sometimes interior, sometimes exterior, and which provides varying instances of spiraling through various plan forms and gaining eight stories in elevation (78–84). We might consider this a parallel for the modern experience of the art museum. If the four courtyards were made as an interior, one would begin to have something very similar to both the spirit and structure of the interior spatial and circulation systems of the Taiyuan Art Museum. Both buildings are wrapped by a surface that tends to conceal the complexities within. The Hohenzollern is the more single-minded geode, although the explosion of the interior elements above its ramparts essentially negates this feature. The Taiyuan Museum is a geode as well, though one that is more about the experience charted by one's movement through the building and the unfolding spatial relationships that occur as a result. It really is the Castle Hohenzollern of China, or perhaps more correctly, the Castle Cohenzollern.

Regardless of the contemporary dress of the Cohen art museum, the beauty of the scheme is its ability to perform. It performs not particularly by way of style, but by its ability to deal with its site, organize its program, and choreograph the experience into something that is so full of surprises, difference, and variety. It is held together not only by the all-enclosing surface of the perimeter, but also by a multitude of interior systems, pieces, spaces, vistas, and experiences that are strung together along its intriguing pathways, which organize and orchestrate the transformations from bottom to top. There may eventually be great art in the building, but to some degree it will hardly make any difference. The building, and particularly the layers of relationships produced by experiencing it, is already one of the best shows in town.

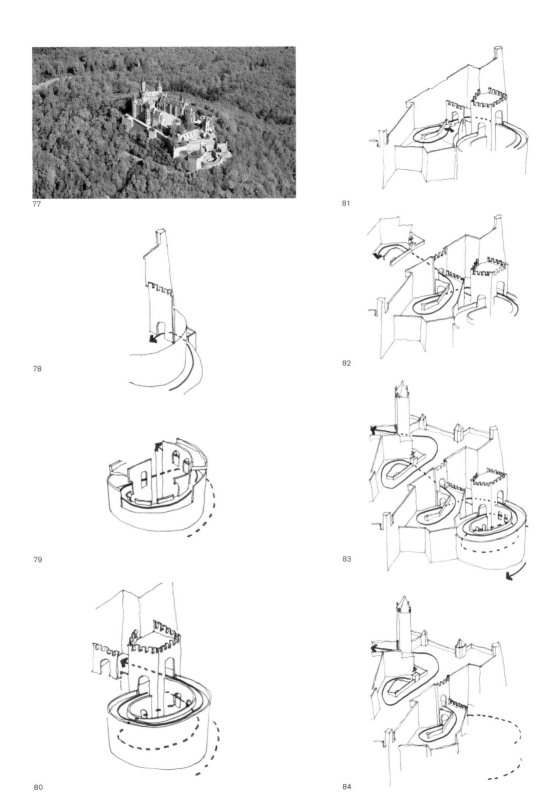

77

78

79

80

81

82

83

84

Interview with Jeffrey Kipnis

The following are edited exerpts from an interview with Jeffrey Kipnis.

BENAJMIN WILKE: The goal of the Baumer Professorship is to recognize practitioners who've made contributions and generated important conversations in architecture and design. Another goal is to expose our students to these practitioners in an intimate setting. The publication series is called Source Books in Architecture, which assumes that we get to the root of the projects and to the larger agenda. So the first question is really more of a prompt and a general cue to start the discussion. What is it for you that makes Scott's work both particular and important?

JEFFREY KIPNIS: I've known Scott since he was a student.

The answer to the question has two parts that would divide his career in half. For the first half of his career, I would say that Scott was the purest design researcher of his generation. I mean this in that he engaged in design analysis of historic and contemporary works and design processes that felt like they had the least obligation to cultural theory justification. He felt that the internal formal regime was sufficient to motivate a speculation about architectural processes. This set him apart from other people in his generation that were deriving a lot of work from theoretical readings and the like. He was a student of Peter Eisenman's and definitely a protégé of Peter's thinking. But Peter would justify a lot of his formal research with arguments derived from cultural theory. Actually, they were closer to Scott in the sense that they were born in the formal properties of the analyses and Scott was the closest of anybody to doing that. When the computer became a valid tool, he was able to continue the work digitally at a very high level in the same regard. This made him unique. For me, it made him the most interesting person of his generation and a little bit of a throwback because I felt like we needed to rethink the self-justified formal

processes. I wanted architectural theory and discourse—and I'm collapsing a lot of the time here—to make a claim for effects beyond the quotidian building effects. I was interested, not in cultural reasons, but in the performance of effects that were not associated with the performance of the building type.

WILKE: That's interesting because for as long as I've known you your approach as a critic has been so heavily interdisciplinary. Yet Scott's project seems almost mono-disciplinary.

KIPNIS: Absolutely.

WILKE: So by Berlin's standards he was a hedgehog, not a fox.

KIPNIS: Absolutely, completely. But then, as he became more and more interested in building, he skipped an entire scale of architectural thinking and became very interested in the process of professional building, I'm not talking about value structures of context and client, necessarily. He just became very interested in what it was to have an office and to build. There's a whole scale at which you became more interested in the process of the material construction and naturally begin to tackle cost, client, and internal performance of the program. He became very practice-oriented, but in a way that didn't derive from an interdisciplinary, cultural discourse. He became extreme in a different way and that's why his relationship with Stan Allen is so very interesting: they interlace with one another and they bracket one another. Stan wanted to build. I think he began as a builder. But he was also always a thinker—a really deep thinker—in all the ways that I thought were correct for that generation. I always thought he was the most interesting thinker and got more and more interesting as a designer. So they were opposites. There's a whole bunch of discussion missing from Scott's work. For example, he did this wonderful lecture on the five points of architecture. I don't know if you've heard it or seen it.

WILKE: We talked about it a little bit when he was here.

KIPNIS: He thinks of the ribbon window as the outlier of the five points. When I teach the five points, the ribbon window is the thing that holds everything together. This is because I teach the five points as holding together as a political discourse. I teach it as a formula for disestablishing ground as land and reestablishing it as datum. Scott sees it entirely as a building operation where the ribbon window is a formal issue that he cannot reconcile with the structure or with the other elements. It's an amazing lecture. It's a totally transforming idea and it shows the complete idiosyncrasy of his thinking with respect to architectural theory. That's an obsession with building, you know? It's about really wanting to find out what one can do in a building *as* a building without the additional interdisciplinary baggage. Did you know that the lightfall in Tel Aviv (1) was expendable at one point? He had to be talked back into keeping it by his friends, myself included.

WILKE: Well, the lightfall is interesting—in part— because it has prior manifestations in earlier work. Lightfall-like elements have been present in his work in some form or another going back to the Cornered House.

KIPNIS: The lightfall, by the way, was never a lightfall. The idea of even calling that thing a lightfall or of thinking of it as a lightfall…I'm sorry about this because I know I'm going to wander a little bit. My job as a critic is not to understand what the architect did and make it understandable or palatable or defend it to other people. I will do that on occasion, but my job as a critic is to look at the work and see it in a light that is totally different from the architect. There are architects that I don't write about very often because what they say about their work is all that I can see in the work. If I can't make myself see something else, I don't write about it. This doesn't mean that I like it or that I don't like it. Bernard Tschumi is an architect that I really love, but he has the uncanny ability to make a building do

1

exactly what he says it does, and that's all I can see and I can't see anything else. I ended up saying that he's the best theoretical architect there is because he does exactly what he says. So when I think about Tel Aviv and the building we're here to talk about today, I don't discuss it at all according to the terms under which Scott presents it because he discusses it very clearly for himself and it's easy to understand. I see something totally different going on in it. I understood the lightfall very early. I knew how it came out of the process, I knew what happened, and I knew what effect I thought it was going to present in the building. I knew what it added to the discussion of museums relative to Richard Meier or Frank Lloyd Wright. I knew that it would be about the psychology of paying attention to art. When you go to Tel Aviv and you see the constellation of lights on the floor you can't *not* like it.

I would argue that he was equally interested—maybe even *more* interested, if only subconsciously—in what happens when you rotate an orthographic volume in digital space plastically instead of tectonically. Normally, you would rotate a piece tectonically or you would rotate it formally and you wouldn't bend anything. When you start rotating a cube in digital space and you allow the plasticity of the digital primitive to bend … that's what it's about. All of the projects, that's what they did. There's a place that they bend and there's a place that they don't bend. They don't bend where they're not fixed or where they're not intersected and that's where you get these corner rotations. He skins these corner rotations so that when you're inside the building, you're inside a space that has corners and you pay attention to the art in one way. When you leave that space, you enter into what would be the circulation element in the Guggenheim museum. What I predicted would happen is that the change in the geometry would cause you to change moods. It would be like the intermission between acts. Museums and curators have a great deal of difficulty understanding the need to modulate attention. Attention fatigue is one of the more disastrous effects of most museums. This is one of the things that neoclassical museums deal with incredibly well by way of size and scale. It is also because of the hall—not the hallways—and how spaces are arranged in relation to it. You need the hall and its thresholds and sequences; you can't *not* have that.

WILKE: The hierarchical spaces create the difference needed to act as a sort of palette cleanser to the experiences and stimuli?

KIPNIS: Yeah. The Guggenheim in New York is relentlessly monotonic in terms of the attention it demands, which is why everybody turns around after two cycles. The nice thing about the lightfall is that it maintains a real continuity while you can continue to see the art. I thought it was an incredible solution for this problem with museums because this is what comes out of good formal research. And then I got there and there were bad things and good things: handrails, interrupted effects, etcetera. But there were so many things that I discovered were going to happen depending on how they installed shows. Some things were going to be really bad for shows and some things were going to be really good for shows.

WILKE: Scott talked about how there has already been a change in curators at Tel Aviv. He said that a new curator came in and talked about new ambitions for that space and they were totally different from the initial curator. At first he was appalled by the idea, but then realized that buildings have second and third lives.

KIPNIS: Yeah, that's what happens in buildings. At the Neue Nationalgalerie, almost immediately after it opened, they started putting art upstairs. It wasn't until the late 1980s that a curator came in and said that it wasn't going to happen anymore. He said that if anything were to be put upstairs, it would be art that's on the floor. They weren't going to put fake walls upstairs in order to install art up there. Did he put the art downstairs because he was waiting for a time when it could be put upstairs? Did he put the art downstairs to protect the operatic status of the museum? These become really interesting questions. Artists have done shows there that make the declaration that you *can* go upstairs, but that there's a certain way to do it. Tel Aviv is fantastic until you get there and then the context is so debilitating as to be dispiriting.

WILKE: The plaza with all of the other buildings along its edge?

KIPNIS: It's just horrible and there's no way to survive going in and coming out. I couldn't survive it again. I wouldn't go back. It is a great building, but only because I keep bracketing out all of the other nightmares. I think Taiyuan is a fantastic building. Look at the vistas and the scales that he had to adjust to in order to adapt some of those same strategies. This is a thing I really love about Scott and you can see it in the new work: you can see him responding to these concerns. The thing about Scott is that he's a great architect, but some of his projects are bad. One thing that concerns me a little bit about certain architects is that there's a uniformly good result. They're not trying stuff, you know? Scott has showed me some work before—you can ask him—and I just told him it was terrible. The competition entry for the Stockholm Library…(2)?

WILKE: There's a bunch of work from that period where he's working with these tendrils of circulation. It's a theme. So maybe they're aborted or failed experiments from the laboratory, but—

KIPNIS: And they got better. No, no, no! That's the point. What I'm saying is that I watch him work on a problem and he has an intuition about things and he works and he works and he works and then it turns out to produce something. That's really what you want. You want somebody who doesn't care that each project is good. You want someone who cares about the fact that they have this idea that they want to work on it and they keep working on it.

WILKE: So lightfall has these Guggenheim-esque, experiential qualities…

KIPNIS: What happens for me is that it manipulates the mood in a way that the Guggenhiem doesn't. If there's a quality to the light, it's because it's casual or accidental. And that's exactly what you want in a museum. You want to walk in there and know that you don't have to think about anything. You're not paying attention to the light, you're not paying attention to the geometry, you're not thinking about the concept. With Eisenman, you would have to be thinking about the concept. In this case, Taiyuan is so big. Things like the entry cantilever are heroics that have to do with the client; that is just Scott being a smart architect for a client. I think it's just more technique that he's developing. It's much more evolved than Tel Aviv.

WILKE: I think this project is the evolution of an idea. You occupy the spaces in a different way; they're different kinds of space. They're not extensions from a center. They're a series of spaces that emerge along a path. It was funny, Rob Livesey and I were doing a pretty thorough walk-through of the drawings for the building and there aren't any sections of it because they'd be almost useless. There is no traditional section.

KIPNIS: There is no section. What is a work of art in a space like that? It's just pointless. It's like putting a work of art in an airport. And yet, this is perfect for a new Chinese museum.

WILKE: Why so?

KIPNIS: Because it's an imperial monument. I mean, they're not quite there yet and they're not yet ready to form intimate relationships to their art collections, but China is in an early imperial phase. These are the spoils of their success, just like the Pergamon Museum. Have you been there?

WILKE: I haven't.

KIPNIS: It's like the British National Museum, or the Met in New York. It's gigantic. When you're in there, part of the experience is knowing how vast it is. The Pergamon is huge. You can put both of Scott's museums in that museum. These are not unusual things for successful countries to do.

WILKE: Taiyuan is an old city, but this city center is going to be an instant production. There are a large number of similar developments across China.

KIPNIS: Right. And this is not going to be the most important imperial museum. But one thing you know is that Scott's not thinking about this. He's got the program and he's got the size. No matter what, he couldn't have done much about that. I think that he did a good job of adapting to what he was working with in this situation. I think the exterior circulation thing is fantastic. He didn't have that possibility in Tel Aviv. I don't think it was part of the program at all. I think he created that as one way he could advance the work on these geometries. He's almost done working on this geometry. This is close to being the last of these projects. He's really trying to work out these windows though.

WILKE: I think that's one of the more curious elements.

KIPNIS: Well, he just does it. The windows have to be congruent with the panelization, right? If you look at Tel Aviv, this newer project deals with the windows much better.

That means he's looked at it. He's probably done a thousand different variations. At Tel Aviv, it's annoying. Those triangular windows look like they really don't belong. But there's nothing he can do about it, he has to do triangle windows.

WILKE: A necessary evil…

KIPNIS: There's no way to poke a hole in the structure. These are gigantically difficult problems at the level of a building. They're part of the building, but not really part of the bigger project.

WILKE: Fine. But when we look at a newer building like the Datong Library, I do think he's accounting for the window as part of the project (3). It's a part of the mosaic that makes up the surface.

And you think he's done with this geometry?

KIPNIS: Well, I think he's worked out almost all of the problems.

WILKE: Do you know his office? The little building in Cambridge? He pretty much had to deal with issues other than formal gymnastics in that renovation.

KIPNIS: Yeah, I know that building. The apartment in that building is great. He tries little phenomenological tricks and this thing is fantastic. He analyzed the site and the structure and it's almost at the limit of tolerance. This is exactly what I did not think he would ever be doing as a professional practitioner. This is all about taking a building apart, looking at the structure, and looking at what tactical performances he can get. No formal anything. It's about getting as many episodes of tactical performance and phenomenological event that you can.

That comes from Harvard, you know? At Harvard you're not trained to think about architecture as a research practice. You acknowledge the existence of people like Danny Liebeskind that do experimental architecture, but you don't really care what their reasons are and you don't care about the discourse. You are trained to see if they produce anything that can be appropriated for a good professional practice. They are experts at building. They can look at something that Liebeskind or Eisenman did and they can build it a lot better and make it perform tricks for clients. That's what Harvard is. It really is an applied design school. So—and you can write this down—what was incredibly interesting about Scott was that he started his architectural life totally enamored by pure research. And he was so good at it that he did these incredible analyses that no one could follow, not even Peter Eisenman.

He stayed in the school whose culture was application and he mastered that. He synthesized these two approaches in an incredible way without any conflict. He's mastered it so much so that now he is very much leaning toward the pleasures of the application and it's produced something very difficult. Of all the architects I follow—and there are a lot of them—I don't know anyone who's ever produced something so singular in their work and that makes so much sense as his Eyebeam competition entry. Scott did it and no one was surprised; it made perfect sense. Yet, no one knew where it came from and no one knew where it was going. I kind of knew where it came from because I knew the analyses that it referenced, but it was a piece of pure research that became a competition entry (4).

WILKE: It was my favorite of the finalists.

KIPNIS: I didn't expect to see it again. I didn't expect it to be part of a line of research. I wouldn't be surprised to see it show up again. But to this day, no project is as different from a body of work as that project is from everything else that Scott has done.

WILKE: Well, he did have the Wu House.

KIPNIS: But you'll see that in early adopter architects:

people like Mack Scoggin and Merrill Elam. In the middle of all the work you can find some incredible, weird, totally postmodern things. They're anomalies. When you look at the analysis that produced it and at the thinking behind it, that project of Scott's is an amazing project and no one actually knows what to make of it. It's hard to write about and hard to discuss. It's fantastic.

WILKE: Yeah. It's a great project. When he was here, he opened the sessions by telling the story about the day that he was supposed to interview with you and Rob.

KIPNIS: I wanted him here. There was no question I wanted him here.

WILKE: He said he was pretty young.

KIPNIS: He *was* young. And you know, Rob Livesey hired me and he brought in everyone I wanted to hire: Jesse Reiser, Greg Lynn, etcetera. Many of these people did some of their best work here. Scott would have fit.

WILKE: Yeah, absolutely.

KIPNIS: He loved it here. He took Doug Graf to teach at Harvard. He'd have fit in here and there'd have been no problem. But you can ask Rob Livesey about that—it was probably bad enough to have me here.

He probably would have hired him. I remember asking why we were doing the formal interview at all. Why don't we just hire him? Then Rafael Moneo called him.

WILKE: I have two more questions.

KIPNIS: Okay.

WILKE: Scott told us he left here and did a sort of grand tour of these villas in Europe. He said the one that did it—that sparked his interest in distortion—was Villa Tauro. Everything kind of began with this.

KIPNIS: Oh, I see. I remember this (5).

WILKE: It's a little villa where the architect has to insert

2 Stockholm Library Competition, Preston Scott Cohen, 2006

3 Datong Library, Preston Scott Cohen, 2008-14

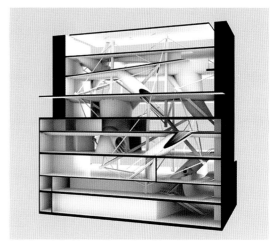

4 Eyebeam Atelier Museum, Preston Scott Cohen, 2001

a band of circulation in a house that's already divided into perfect thirds. In some ways, it screws everything up. Scott talks about this project in conjunction with the Holbein skull and the beginning interests in anamorphism. I think it's really interesting that the ideas about distortion came from this project.

KIPNIS: See, that's fantastic. It's real obvious. What I love about it is that the architect is totally unashamed of it.

WILKE: Right.

KIPNIS: "Well, what else was I gonna do?"

WILKE: Exactly.

KIPNIS: It's like that little window in San Carlo.

WILKE: Scott talked about that as well.

KIPNIS: You look at it and think, "I gotta have a window right there."

WILKE: Well, he talks about that project and how he realized that projection can be functional and do architectural work beyond experimentation and research.

KIPNIS: And was there a question about that? That's how we were taught to think. We were taught to go find these things, you know?

WILKE: It was more about how these discoveries also led to his thinking about circulation and procession. This is another prominent element in Scott's work, right? It's always just as much about procession and circulation.

KIPNIS: Of all the people of that generation, he and Stan remain plan driven – Scott probably a little more so. Did he do his analysis of Koolhaas's ZKM when he was here?

WILKE: No. But he talked about how he never understood the love for that project until he understood what the Vierendeel truss allows it to do.

KIPNIS: He begins Tel Aviv by looking at how every floor in ZKM is a different world. That's how those rotations are supposed to produce different worlds that stay connected. There was an idea about producing the most difference with the greatest coherence. It's an idea related to a quote from Leibnitz that shows up in Deleuze as being about multiplicity. That was the only time that I've ever suggested—and he didn't know this until later—that he was being Deleuzian.

WILKE: Which he would never consciously be.

KIPNIS: He just said no. He asked why there couldn't simply be pure formal research.

WILKE: There's definitely a mad scientist quality. You have the explorations and the aborted experiments. I would put Greg Lynn in that category too.

KIPNIS: Yeah. But to stay obsessed with the plan and to analyze the plan? There was a real drift away from the plan across the discipline. The idea of the plan as generator had been rejected; it was either section or diagram. Then people started to debate what a diagram was. Villa Tauro, though—that's a great project.

WILKE: Last topic: Scott said that early in his thinking, he recognized that architects always try to define what architecture is. The students pressed him on what he thought the most accurate declarations were. We went through the list: "What the brick wants to be," "Less is more," etcetera. He named Philip Johnson's definition of architecture as being the art of wasting space. He also mentioned affinity with Le Corbusier's claim that architecture happens when the window is too big or too small.

KIPNIS: I have three problems with the first declaration: *art*, *wasting*, and *space*. These add up to make a fantastic quip, but nobody can say what they are. What do you mean by *art*? What do you mean by *wasting*? What do you mean by *space*? I think Kristy Balliet's work on *Excessive Volume* is the most original contribution to this topic since these other definitions that you mention. I think the discipline is ready for someone to give us an answer—you hear me say this a lot. I'm sure her intuition may be correct in *not* answering it. But to be able to become precise about what volume, void, and space are, and to allow the discipline to become more articulate and agile on these issues, is extremely exciting. Sorry, I just got done reading this article about weather.

WILKE: Right. You were telling me about that.

KIPNIS: The biggest thing for establishing the proper discipline of meteorology was for them to find the vocabulary. There were a lot of efforts to find a vocabulary and none of them produced anything that they could use. When they finally found a vocabulary that could, for example, describe a cloud, and was repeatable—*you'll* love this—there was a problem because a lot of the terms were just too metaphoric. The problem with metaphors is that they have strengths and weaknesses and one of the weaknesses is how quantifiable they can or can't be. Everything starts as descriptive language and it took a long time to figure this out. There was a breakthrough when some guy named the clouds in a way that was descriptive and, more importantly, measurable. For example, "curl" and "mass." It turns out that you can measure a curl or a mass. *Nimbus* and *cumulus* were the Latin words for those. These terms lent themselves to repetition and measurement enough that they became the technical terms for a proper science. So I do think the art of wasting space is a useful quip but—

WILKE: It's about purposefully making inefficiencies, right? It's about producing elements or spaces that are outside of the norm for the sake of some impact, be it experiential or—

KIPNIS: What I'm saying is that we all knew what it meant when we saw it, yet no one knew how to teach it. Really talented people knew how to do it or knew it when they saw it, but it didn't really help the discipline much. Whereas everyone can quickly teach someone to read when a window is too big or too little. You know, the lifetime of a building *as* a building is about twenty-five years. I think that's always true, even with cathedrals and things that might take 100 years to build. Liturgy, generations, and politics might last twenty-five or fifty years, but the people in those practices are gone in the first generation or two. The minute a building is orphaned, whatever is left that keeps the building thriving as an orphan, *that* is architecture. So it means a lot of things get to be architecture, and you can never

form or get a catalogue from it. Sometimes it will be a big window, sometimes a little window, and sometimes a window that is exactly the right size depending on what just happened. Wasting space is great until you're tired of it. So it's whatever survives the first two generations. What I think is great about someone like Peter Eisenman is that he taught *the profession* of architecture. He would focus the students' entire life on the first and second generation of users. Those are the people that paid for it. The entire practice of the profession had become—for very good reasons—defined by the first twenty-five years of a building. It was for the people that lived in the building and the people that had to see it. Even though they knew from history that their building was going to last longer than that, this is still what mattered. Peter taught them not only to care about that, but how to care about both at the same time. I think that's a big deal, and that's why I think Scott defines his generation. I think everything he does has both considerations in mind.

5

Cohen in Taiyuan

Robert Livesey

April is the cruelest month, breeding
Lilacs out of the dead land, mixing
Memory and desire, stirring
Dull roots with spring rain.
— T.S. Eliot, *The Waste Land*

The context for Preston Scott Cohen's Taiyuan Art Museum in China is a bit of a misery: another of those planned instant city centers trying to be Karlsruhe yet lacking any of the charm or subtlety. Composed of twenty and thirty story buildings, the town is a midrise hell (1). All of the cultural buildings, isolated on an island among wasteland plazas, compete for attention (2). This civic center—with a split city hall, deadly symmetry, and a humongous and out-of-scale water feature—seems to be modeled on Villa Lante or multiple other gardens, but there are no surprises. It is just big.

Cohen is clearly trying to establish the museum in contrast to the context. Although it is a five-story building, one never sees all five floors. The route through the museum would actually encourage one to read it as a single-story building that wraps around itself. The scale is difficult and sometimes impossible to read. Most interesting is the distortion of the floors: the slipping and sliding and insertion of programmatic spaces, the crossovers, the indentations and projections, the bobbing and weaving, the bending, crimping, and arcing. This is where the architecture and the spatial manipulation reside.

Think of ribbons and bows with their loops, knots, and ends. They are all present. There is the gallery ribbon that, in its natural state, is approximately seven short panels high and fourteen long panels wide on the exterior. There is the ramp ribbon that winds its way up through the building and jumps from floor to floor via escalators while disappearing and reappearing, sometimes being deflected only to be found again on the next floor up; it is sometimes consumed by a gallery and sometimes autonomous. At the top, the circulation ribbon continues down a circular stair and through a mezzanine across the garden lobby. From here, one transitions down a small ramp through a sloped gallery and back to the gallery ribbon. The gallery ribbon continues on a crimped path (under the exterior pass-through to the garden court) before folding upon itself and moving back up through the galleries to the garden lobby (3).

The offices on the third floor form a bow and reappear on the fourth floor in a more bulbous form (4). There is an exterior path with a single looped end that moves through and around the building and helps to resolve the axis of the convention/exhibition center and the path to the cultural plaza (5). The proportions of the individual galleries reiterate a long and low ribbon form. Given the distorted form of the building, it is surprising how ribbon-like the galleries are. In fact, the individual galleries form their own independently-scaled piece of ribbon. Ironically, this scale of ribbon is most apparent in the restaurant on the fifth floor where it is bounded by a sloped garden and an outside court (6).

Some galleries do have volume, but always as a distortion of the ribbon form. The gallery to the left of the entrance is a good example. Here, the seven-panel high facade is maintained but bent up to add void volume to the ribbon space while the sloped floor adds additional dimension by dropping below the ground (7).

The classroom ensemble on the first floor is certainly a knot (8) with the garden court galleries functioning as ribbon ends. The library on the second floor is tightly tied. The galleries that surround the third and fourth floor atrium form a loop and one end of a ribbon while, on the fifth floor, the other end of the same ribbon is projected over the entrance (9).

What is clear is that the overall form of the building is a double courtyard or—indeed—a bow. One courtyard is exterior while the other is an interior atrium with an

1

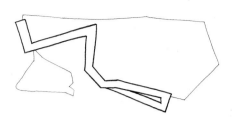

2

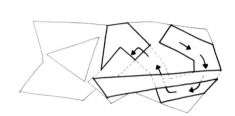

3

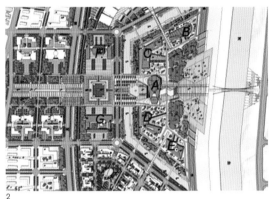

4

5

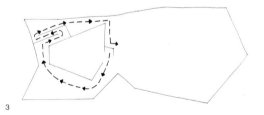

6

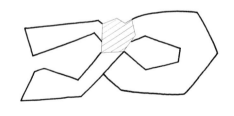

7

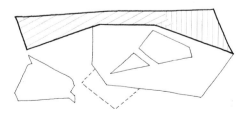

8

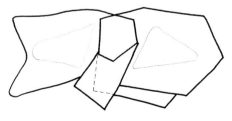

9

exterior garden attached (10). The stepped garden is perhaps a reminder that all of the atrium was once an exterior. The primary radial form of the atrium's skylight is an homage to the Guggenheim skylight in New York while the linear secondary structure lends the impression that the glass roof could be pulled back (11).

A particular strangeness in the building is the punched windows (12). While there is little doubt that they provide necessary and exciting views, it is also difficult to understand how they reinforce or are informed by the logic that occurs elsewhere. The systematic integration of circulation, large-scale glass walls, programming, and spatial organization is gymnastic and indicative of Cohen's mastery of manipulated form. But whereas most of the elements work together to expose the virtues of experiencing distorted space, these windows are a curiosity. They are isolated events, sometimes triangular and sometimes rectangular, but always a panel removed. These instances may reveal the nature of the panels that skin the larger form or they may be small-scale reminders of functional necessities. Ultimately, they lack much of the fluidity and reinforcing nature that the other moves possess.

One of the most remarkable transformations of this form is the 'eyelid' pulled over the outside entry to the exterior courtyard. It is an enormous unused volume that turns the frog-shaped building into a double courtyard. Cohen seems to be playing out an age-old theme of coherence and articulated bits. The same theme appears in the grouping of the galleries and other programmatic pieces around the atrium. If one understands the building—as one can while standing in the atrium—as a voided block, then the roof becomes an enveloping form that covers three separate and articulated pieces that face the atrium. The most articulation happens at the lower levels while things become more coherent as one moves up through the building, culminating in the restaurant that sees all the previously separate pieces fuse into one. A similar condition exists in the exterior courtyard where the galleries and hall are articulated below, but become a single entity at the top.

An important part of the coherence and articulated bits scenario is that the building is a distorted rectangle while the courtyards are triangular. The sharp angles of the triangles allow for a disjunction while the shrink-wrapped skin encourages coherence. The triangular forms also allow for a more active overlap of elements. The last gallery on the fourth floor contains the circular stair and maintains a triangular geometry. It is simultaneously frontal to three spaces: the exterior courtyard, the gallery sequence, and the elevator lobby/stepped garden.

This stapling together of parts happens over and over again. The game seems to be to make elements as different as possible in both form and program and then to staple them back together. On the lower level of the garden court, the galleries are tied together by an underground connection (13a). On the second level, the outside wall holds the disparate galleries together (13b). On the third level, the administration area is halfway in the courtyard wing and halfway in the atrium gallery wing (13c). On the fourth level, the mechanical area next to the garden court is part of a deformed gallery sequence (13d). On the fifth floor, the restaurant 'flyover' keeps the courtyard galleries under its wing (13e).

There are many references for the Taiyuan Museum of Art. The atrium could easily be seen as a riff on I. M. Pei's East Wing of the National Gallery in Washington. The distorted double courtyards might be referencing the Palazzo Medici. The ribbons could refer to the Endless House. The path through the building is reminiscent of Stirling's Stuttgart and LeCorbusier's Carpenter Center. The atrium ramps and skylight recall the Guggenheim in New York. But Cohen is a baroque master and ultimately is interested in making functional yet disrupted space. In Taiyuan, he does it both inside and out. The ability to articulate the layers of panels, the floors, and the overall volume while melding the three of them together is a small indication of his prowess. On the inside, the galleries are allowed to remain relatively normal while the atrium is crunched, stretched, and expanded. The circulation is wrapped around itself by way of being offset, bent, broken, and allowed to wander. If one can imagine that this was once a modernist building that was forced to deal with the vicissitudes of contemporary culture, then it all makes sense: lilacs with spring rain.

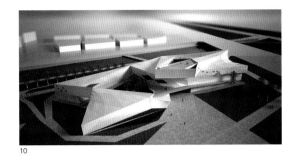

10

11

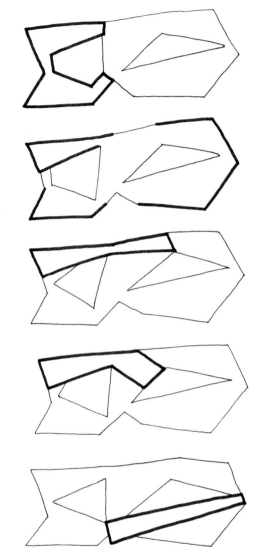

13a–13e

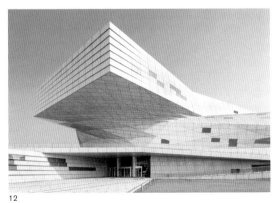

12

TAIYUAN MUSEUM OF ART

Project Description

The Taiyuan Museum of Art works as a cluster of buildings unified by continuous and discontinuous promenades both inside and outside. The building responds to the urban parkscape in which it is set; visitors are encouraged to pass through the building while not entering into the museum itself. An exterior ramp threading through the building connects the heterogeneous hardscapes, lawns and sculpture gardens. The integration of building and landscape registers multiple scales of territory ranging from the enormity of the adjacent Fen River and parkway to the intimacy of the museum's own particular spatial episodes.

Inside, the security of museum space is maintained by a highly controlled interface between gallery and non-gallery programs including an auditorium, bookstore, restaurant, library, education center, and administrative wing. The individual sets of elevators and cores are distributed to guarantee easy access and easy divisibility between zones regulated by different schedules and rules of access. At the garage level, the services are intricately planned in order not to interfere with parking lots for staff and public.

The museum galleries are organized to ensure maximum curatorial flexibility. The galleries can be curated as a single, spiraling itinerary suitable for large chronological exhibitions or as autonomous clusters of exhibitions that are structured independently. The placement of ramps and the proportional expansion and contraction of spaces provide the means of wayfinding. The building provides visitors the freedom either to follow a predetermined chronological sequence or to skip from one set of galleries to another, in a nonlinear fashion. People ascend ramps that spiral around the atrium, weave in and out of galleries, and descend an open staircase that bypasses several levels on its way down to the loop of galleries that surround the large sculpture courtyard.

The facades are composed as hyperbolic parabolas (hypars) that appear to be derived from tilted and twisted parallelograms which rise and fall along with the landscape and exterior ramps. The facade hypars are translated into folded plates. A patchwork of quad-panelized hypars span the facades. Altogether, the building reads as a thick, variably-curved surface, the folded plate edges of which appear to articulate layers.

The concrete structural base of the building is integrated with the parking surrounded on three sides by sloped landscapes rising from waterways. The building is steel framed, culminating in vierendeel trusses supporting the fifteen meter cantilever of the restaurant.

The entire façade and roof are clad in lightweight honeycomb panels with stone veneer that produce an evocative and elusive material effect. On the one hand, the panels are reflective as if they are metal and yet are too perfectly flat to be. On the other hand, their flatness suggests they are clad in stone, though they are seemingly too large to be. The panels clearly possess properties of both materials that are contradicted.

PROJECT CREDITS

Client
Taiyuan City Government

Total Area
32,500 m2

Construction Budget
6,500 RMB/m2

Project Schedule
Winner of the international competition, 2007
Design, 2007-2010
Construction, 2010-2013

Project Team
Preston Scott Cohen, Inc., Cambridge, MA
Preston Scott Cohen (architectural design)
Amit Nemlich (project architect)
Collin Gardner, Hao Ruan, Joshua Dannenberg (project assistants)
Yair Keshet (model)
Architecture Design and Research Institute of South East University,
Taiyuan (architect of record)

Project Design

Preston Scott Cohen Taiyuan Museum of Art

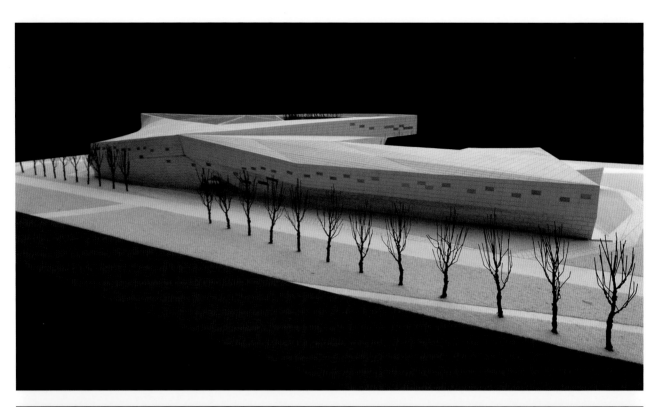

Preston Scott Cohen Taiyuan Museum of Art

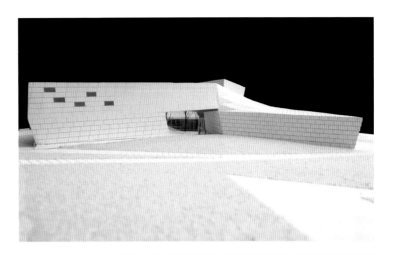

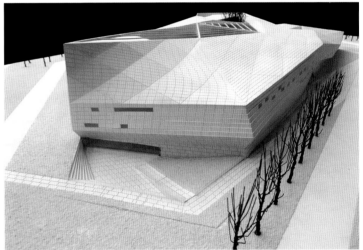

Preston Scott Cohen Taiyuan Museum of Art

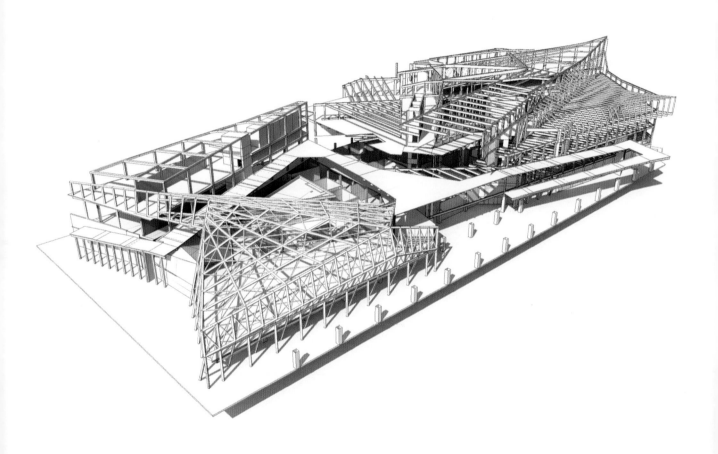

Plans

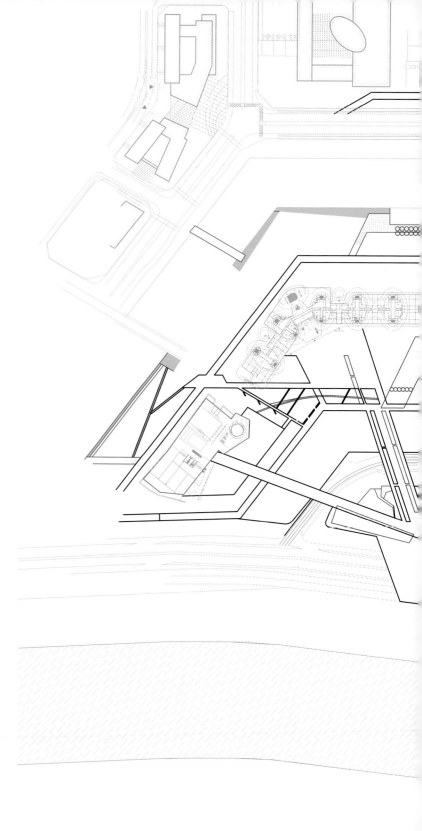

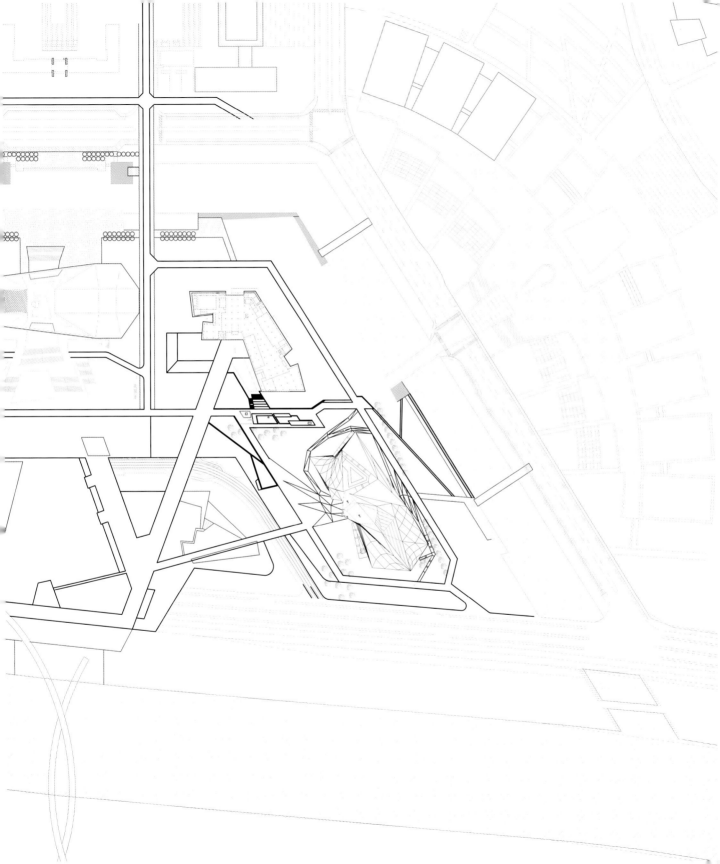

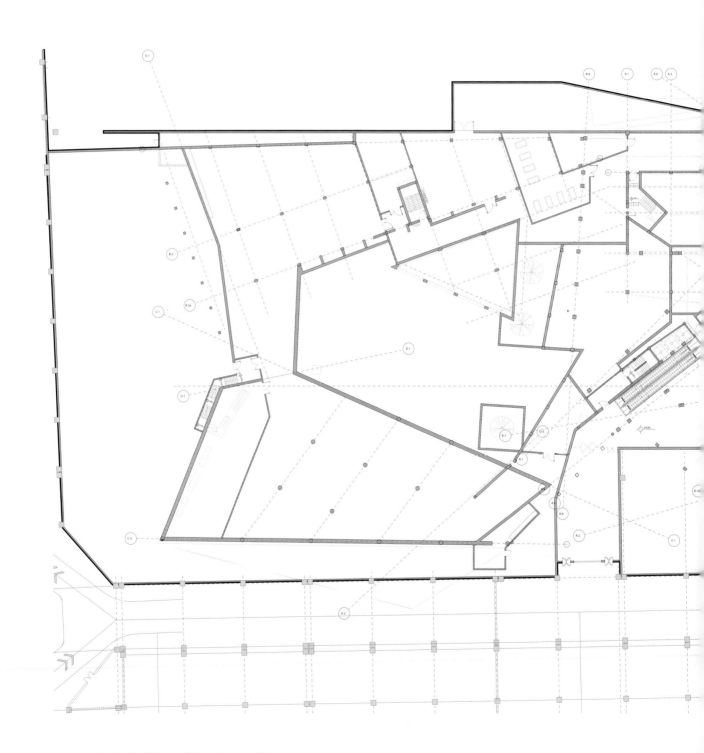

Preston Scott Cohen Taiyuan Museum of Art

00   10M   20M   30M

N

PLAN -01

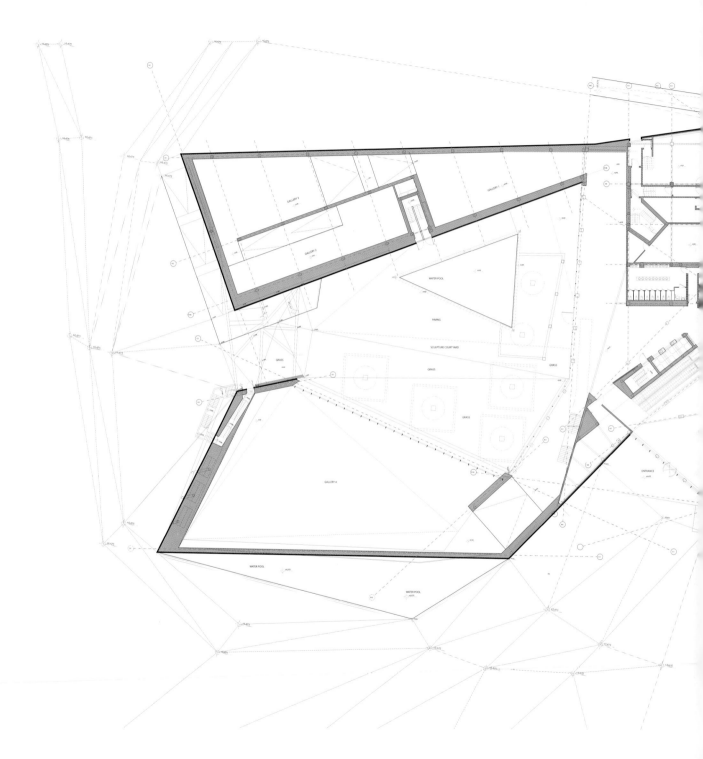

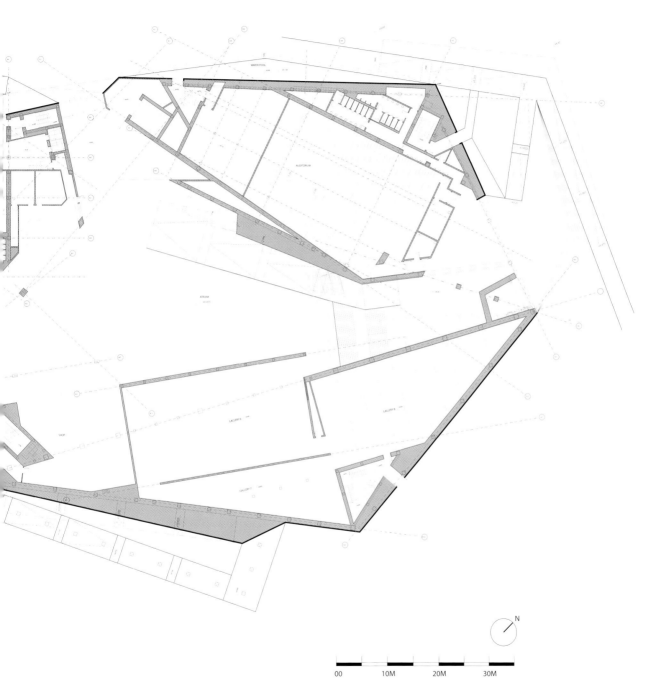

Plan 00A

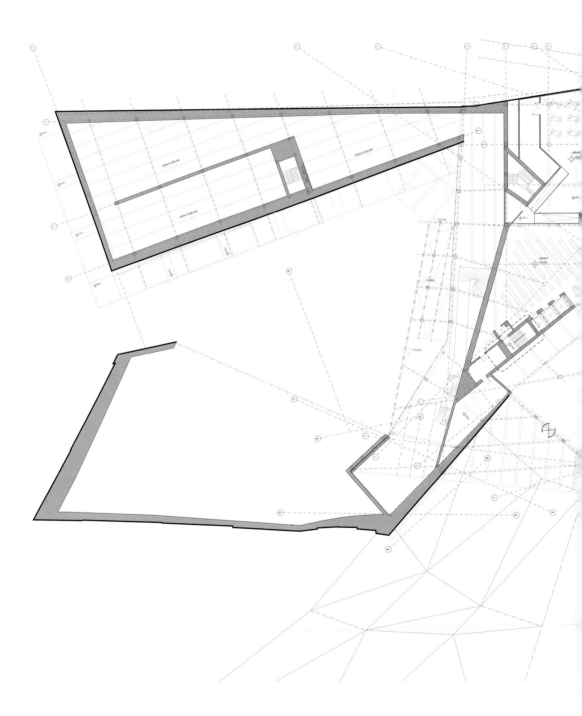

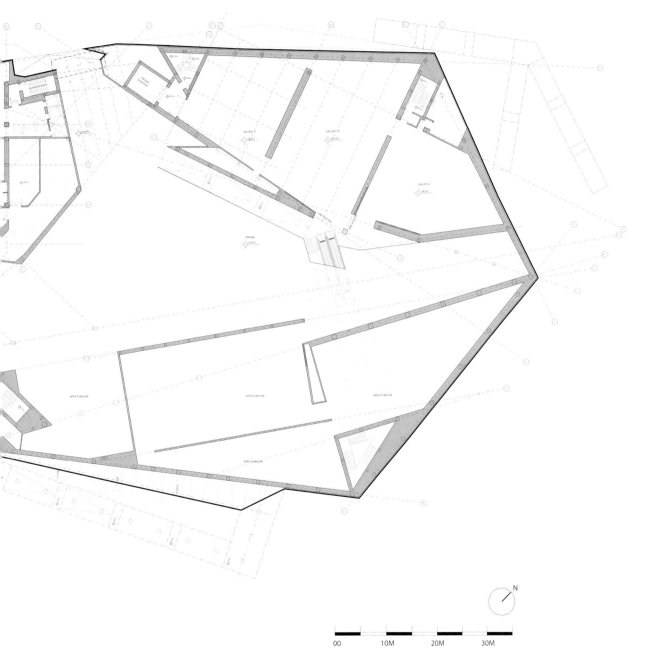

N

00 10M 20M 30M

Plan 01

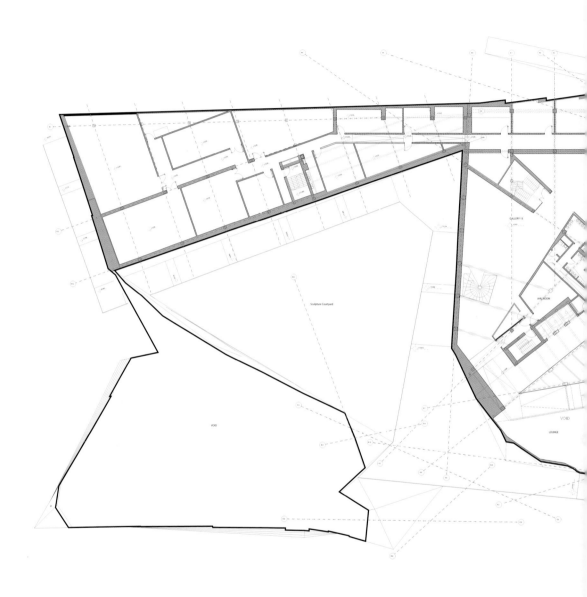

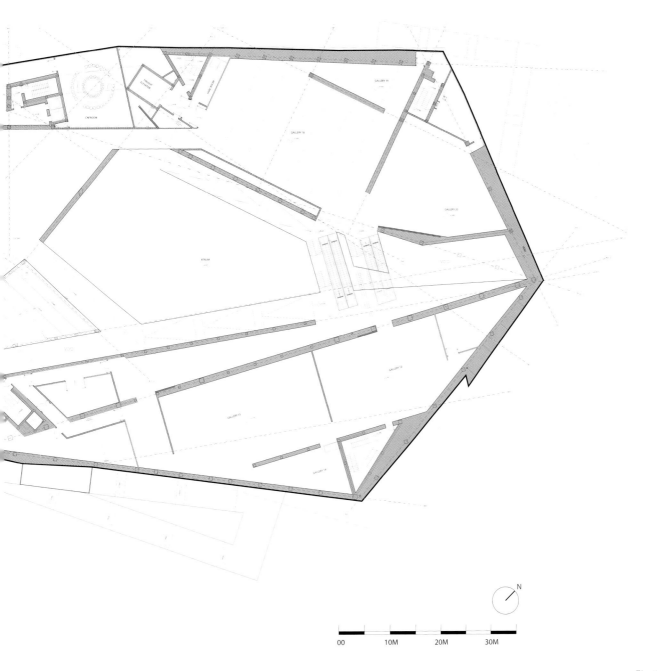

N

00   10M   20M   30M

Plan 02

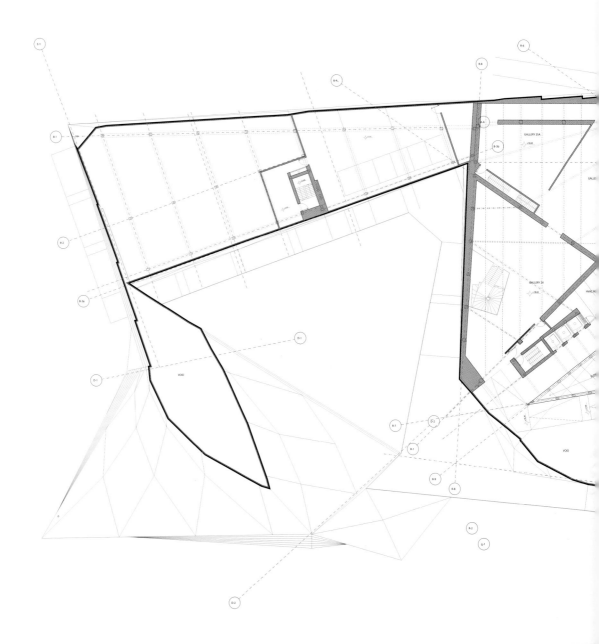

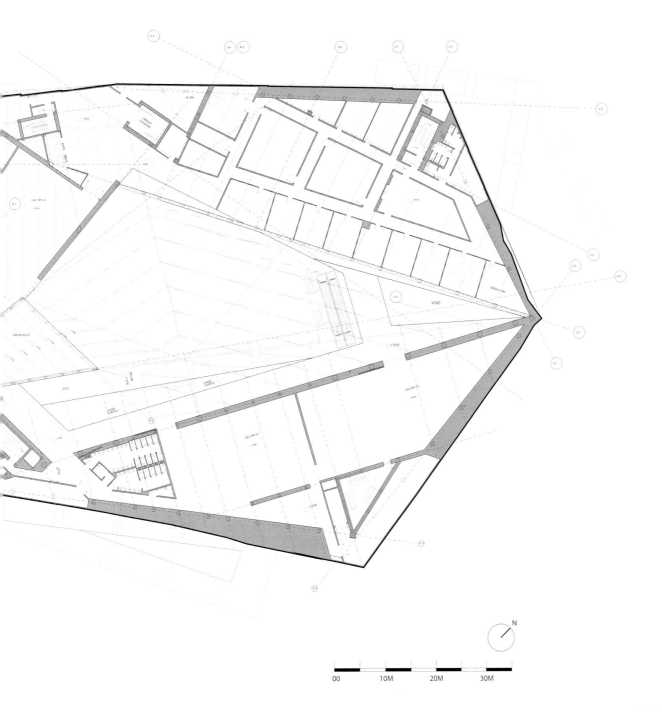

N

00   10M   20M   30M

Plan 03

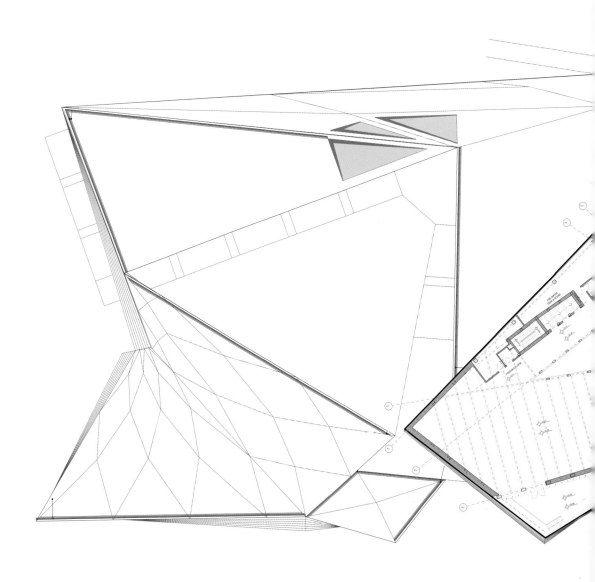

Preston Scott Cohen Taiyuan Museum of Art

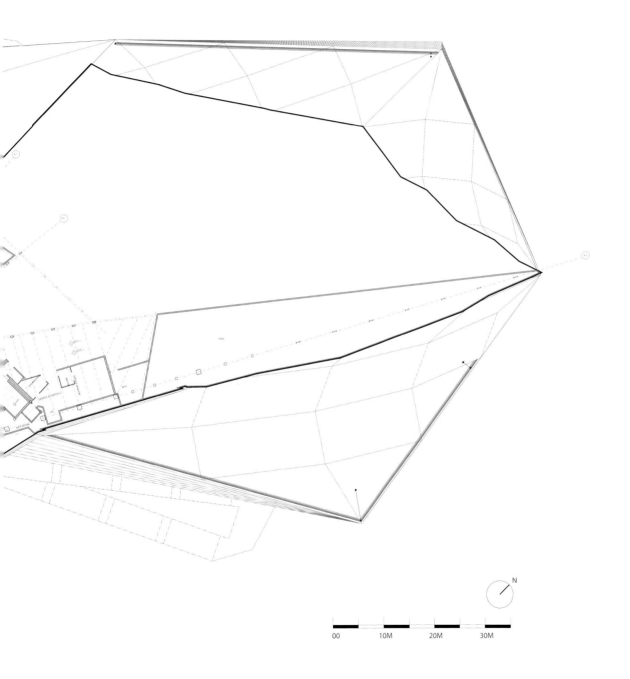

N

00   10M   20M   30M

Plan 04

Construction

Preston Scott Cohen Taiyuan Museum of Art

Built Photos

Preston Scott Cohen Taiyuan Museum of Art

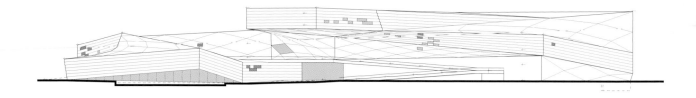

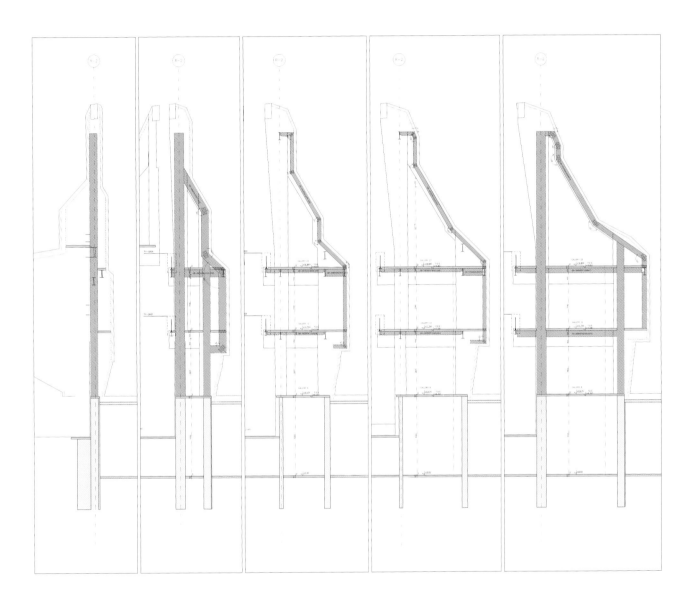

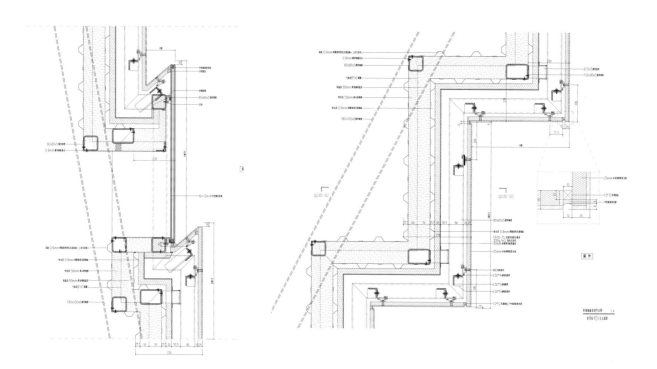

Preston Scott Cohen Taiyuan Museum of Art

Preston Scott Cohen Taiyuan Museum of Art

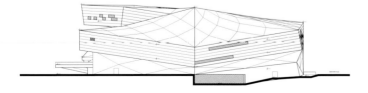

Preston Scott Cohen Taiyuan Museum of Art

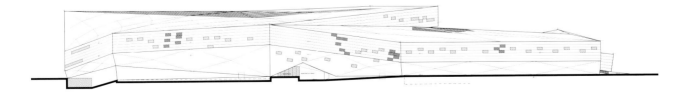

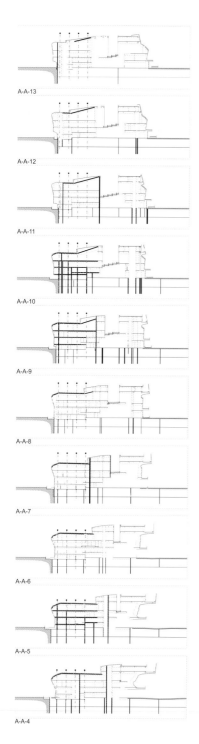

A-A-13

A-A-12

A-A-11

A-A-10

A-A-9

A-A-8

A-A-7

A-A-6

A-A-5

A-A-4

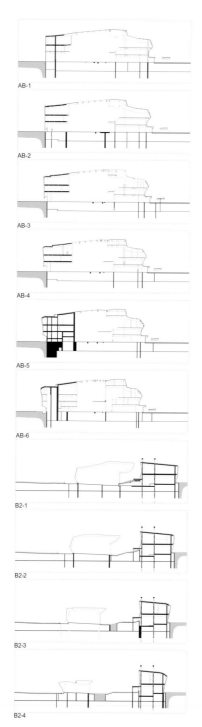

AB-1

AB-2

AB-3

AB-4

AB-5

AB-6

B2-1

B2-2

B2-3

B2-4

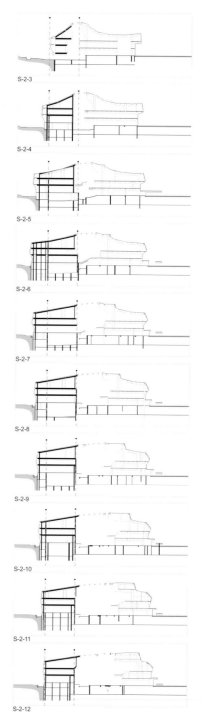

S-2-3

S-2-4

S-2-5

S-2-6

S-2-7

S-2-8

S-2-9

S-2-10

S-2-11

S-2-12

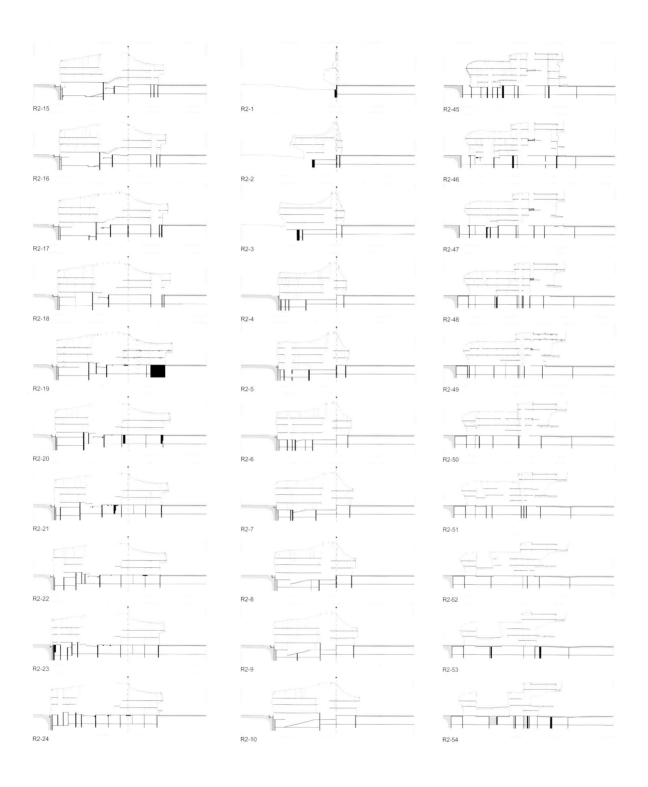

R2-15

R2-16

R2-17

R2-18

R2-19

R2-20

R2-21

R2-22

R2-23

R2-24

R2-1

R2-2

R2-3

R2-4

R2-5

R2-6

R2-7

R2-8

R2-9

R2-10

R2-45

R2-46

R2-47

R2-48

R2-49

R2-50

R2-51

R2-52

R2-53

R2-54

Preston Scott Cohen Taiyuan Museum of Art

Taiyuan Museum of Art 139

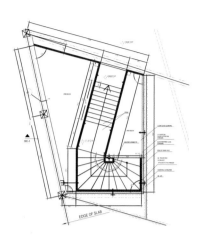

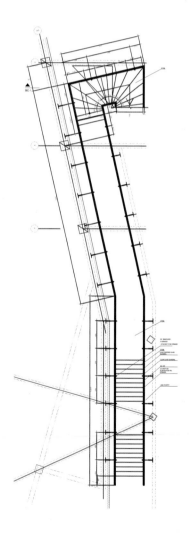

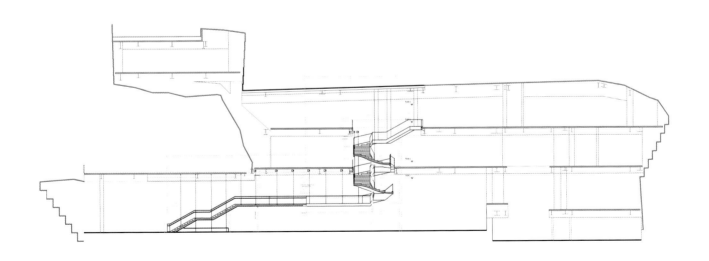

Image Credits

All reasonable efforts have been made to trace the copyright holders of the visual material reproduced in this book. The publisher and the Knowlton School of Architecture apologize to anyone who has not been reached. Errors and omissions will be corrected in future editions.

All images provided by Preston Scott Cohen Inc. except those noted below:

p. 13, middle left: Bad Press: Dissident Ironing, San Francisco, 1993-1998. Photo by Michael Moran. Courtesy of Diller + Scofidio

p. 13, bottom left: Photo by Eric Leishman, © Eric Leishman

p. 15, top right: illustration by Cynthia Klepadlo, Marine Vertebrates Collection, Scripps Institution of Oceanography, UCSD

p. 29, top right: via Library of Congress, Prints & Photographs Division, ILL, 47-PLAN.V, 1-8

p. 31, top left: Venturi and Rauch, Dream House Project, 1974, Jersey Shore, Pennsylvania. Courtesy of Venturi, Scott Brown and Associates, Inc

p. 33, bottom right: Photo by Mary Ann Sullivan, © Mary Ann Sullivan

p. 37, second from bottom: Photo by Raimund Koch

p. 43, top: "Chiswick House (1725-29) by Lord Burlington" by Steve Cadman. Licensed under the Creative Commons Attribution-Share Alike 2.0 Generic license

p. 43, bottom: "M2 Building" by phosphor. Licensed under the Creative Commons Attribution 3.0 Unported license, https://creativecommons.org/licenses/by/3.0

p. 47, top right: Photo by Victoria Sambunaris

p. 47, second from bottom right: via Library of Congress, Prints & Photographs Division, RI, 1-BRIST,18-31

p. 63, second from top left, Courtesy of Zaha Hadid Architects

p. 65, second from top left, Photo by Andreas Yankopolus, © Andreas Yankopolus

p. 65, top right, by Perman, David, A New Guide to Scott's Grotto (Ware, 1995), p.6, © David Perman

p. 75, "Villa Tauro" by GFStellin, © GFStellin

Photos by Amit Geron: p. 18, bottom left; p. 23, middle right; p. 39, top; p. 49, second from top left; p. 69

Photo by Hufton and Crow: p. 23, top right

Photos by Sergio Pirrone: p. 34-35; p. 49, top left, bottom right; p. 77, top left; p. 79 middle left, bottom left; p. 115; p. 116; p. 119; p. 120; p. 122; p. 126-127; p. 128-129; p. 130; p. 134; p. 135; p. 137; p.138; p. 139; p. 140-141; p. 142-143; p. 146-147

Photos by Iwan Baan: p. 49, second from bottom left; p. 124-125; p. 144

Photos by ShuHe Architectural Photography Studio: p. 121; p. 136

Biographies

Benjamin Wilke is the editor of the Source Books in Architecture series and instructor at the Knowlton School of Architecture at Ohio State University, where he teaches design studios and seminars at the undergraduate and graduate level.

Preston Scott Cohen is the Gerald M. McCue Professor in Architecture at Harvard University's Graduate School of Design, where he served as Chair of the Department of Architecture from 2008–2013. An architect with a practice that encompasses diverse scales and types of buildings, he is the author of *Lightfall* (Skira 2016), *The Return of Nature* (with Erika Naginski, Routledge 2015), *Contested Symmetries* (Princeton Architectural Press, 2001), and numerous theoretical and historical essays on architecture. Cohen is the recipient of numerous awards and honors. His work has been widely published and exhibited and is held in numerous museum collections.

Stan Allen is an architect working in New York and George Dutton '27 Professor of Architecture at Princeton University. From 2002 to 2012 he was Dean of the School of Architecture at Princeton. He holds degrees from Brown University, The Cooper Union, and Princeton. His architectural firm *SAA/Stan Allen Architect* has realized buildings and urban projects in the United States, South America, and Asia. His work is published in *Points + Lines: Diagrams and Projects for the City*, (2001) and his essays in *Practice: Architecture, Technique and Representation* (2008). His most recent book is *Landform Building: Architecture's New Terrain*, published in 2011.

Kristy Balliet is co-founder of BairBalliet and principal of Balliet Studio. She is an Assistant Professor at the Ohio State University's Knowlton School of Architecture and a graduate of Philadelphia University and the UCLA Department of Architecture and Urban Design. From 2006-2011, Balliet was an assistant professor at The University of Applied Arts, Vienna in Studio Greg Lynn. From 1999-2006, she practiced architecture in Philadelphia at Erdy McHenry Architecture. She has lectured and exhibited work in San Diego, Philadelphia, Skopje, Vienna, Innsbruck, Berlin, Ann Arbor, New York, and Los Angeles.

Douglas Graf is an architect and urban planner based in Columbus, Ohio. He is a Professor of Architecture at the Knowlton School of Architecture and a frequent visiting critic at institutions worldwide. His writings have appeared in *The Use and Abuse of Paper* (1999), *DATUTOP*, *ANY*, and elsewhere.

Jeffrey Kipnis is Professor of Architecture at the Knowlton School of Architecture. He is widely known for his writing, teaching, and curatorial activities, which include the exhibitions, *Mood River* and *Perfect Acts of Architecture*, and the documentary film, *A Constructive Madness*. A collection of his essays, *A Question of Qualities*, has recently been published by the MIT Press.

Robert Livesey is Professor of Architecture at the Knowlton School of Architecture. In 1983, Livesey came to Ohio State to become Chair of the Department of Architecture, a role he held until 1991. From 1997 to 2005, he served as the Director of the Knowlton School of Architecture. Livesey served as interim head of the Landscape Architecture Section from 2011 to 2013. Currently, he is head of the Architecture Section. He is a Fellow of the American Institute of Architects and of the American Academy in Rome.